HAUNTED
BRIGHTON

HAUNTED
BRIGHTON

ALAN MURDIE

TEMPUS

Frontispiece: *Brighton Aquarium and Palace Pier.*

First published 2006
Reprinted 2007

Tempus Publishing
Cirencester Road, Chalford,
Stroud, Gloucestershire, GL6 8PE
www.tempus-publishing.com

Tempus Publishing is an imprint of NPI Media Group

British Library Cataloguing in Publication Data.
A catalogue record for this book is available from the British Library.
Typesetting and origination by NPI Media Group

ISBN 978 07524 3829 0

CONTENTS

ACKNOWLEDGEMENTS

I would like to express my grateful thanks to a considerable number of people for help in writing *Haunted Brighton*.

In particular, I would like to thank photographer Anna Pearce for her hard work and braving the elements on cold January days to capture the photographs of modern-day Brighton contained in this book.

Locally a great many people assisted with my enquiries in Brighton itself. These include the staff at Brighton Public library, Brighton Town Hall and the Brighton police. Particular thanks go the many friendly and helpful staff of numerous pubs, hotels and public buildings who answered my enquiries. In particular, I must also mention Martin Feuersteiner for sharing his many local contacts and knowledge., and also Glenda Clarke. Thanks are also due to Andy Frame, Rob Spencer, Jo Pratt, Andi Frost and Pauline Davy. Mrs Kathy Gearing, chair of the Ghost Club, also shared her contacts and Mr Lionel Gibson helped me with details of his experience at the Druid's Head Inn.

Special thanks must also go to the late Andrew Green, the veteran ghost hunter who first got me interested in this subject and also grateful thanks to his widow Norah Green for permission to use his unpublished notes and materials. Many thanks are extended to writer Stewart Evans who secured a number of rare pictures for me which are reproduced herein and to historian Robert Halliday for much advice and practical help with obtaining illustrations. Particular thanks are due to Michelle Bird for her invaluable help in locating certain literary references. I would also like to express my thanks to the late Dennis Bardens for maintaining and bequeathing to me a unique scrapbook of press cuttings in which a number of Brighton ghost stories were discovered.

Staff at the following libraries also generously gave help whenever needed: Bury St Edmunds Record Office, Collindale Newspaper Library (scene of a number of serendipitous finds), Lewes Records Office, Cambridge University Library and the Library of the Society for Psychical Research.

On the production side I must thank Matilda Pearce and Ed Palmer of Tempus Books for answering with patience my technical queries which eased the course of this book and for their encouragement with the project, and also Paul Newman for the illustration of the phantom vessel in Chapter Six, which was taken from his book *Haunted Cornwall* (2005).

INTRODUCTION

Brighton is often unfairly thought of as a comparatively new town and therefore lacking in ghosts. Although little more than a fishing village until the mid-eighteenth century, the future Brighton certainly had history, as archaeologists and historians will confirm, as Brighthelmstone. By the beginning of the nineteenth century the town was expanding rapidly, its growth stimulated by the passion for sea bathing and the building of the Pavilion and Dome. Thereafter, Brighton has seldom looked back and for nearly two centuries its name has been inextricably associated with holidays, relaxation and fun.

It is possible that this progressive, fun-filled atmosphere did not encourage ghost stories – other than rides on the Pier Ghost Train. However, it was really the preconceptions of the authors of popular ghost books which led to Brighton hauntings being neglected. Many compilers of ghost books simply followed the late Victorian obsession for hauntings in royal residences, stately homes and ancient castles. Modern seaside resorts such as Brighton and its environs do not immediately fit the haunted heritage image and were overlooked as a result. But over the years there have been ghosts and hauntings aplenty in Brighton and many of them are very well attested indeed.

The first major effort to document Brighton hauntings was undertaken in the 1950s by Robert Thurston Hopkins, a most entertaining but regrettably sometimes inaccurate writer. Brighton ghosts merited a chapter by Frank Usher in *50 Great Ghost Stories* (1971) but a more serious and scientific approach to the area awaited the research of my friend the late Andrew Green, active in ghost investigation for some sixty years. Andrew Green wrote up a number of hauntings in his books and personally investigated many more locally. Another very substantial catalogue of local hauntings was undertaken by writer John Rackham for his excellent *Brighton Ghosts, Hove Hauntings*, published in 2001. All these authors deserve credit and gratitude for helping redressing the historical neglect of Brighton's ghosts and I hope this book will play a small part in maintaining such interest.

This book encompasses not only Brighton ghosts but also some of the hauntings from nearby Hove and the surrounding district. Herein will be found, in Chapter One, ghost stories from Brighton's famous Lanes. A selection of stories involving genuinely haunted private homes appears in Chapter Two, detailing cases spread over more than a century. The phantoms of bygone celebrities at the Pavilion, the Dome and the Theatre Royal are examined in Chapter Three, whilst Chapter Four details some of Brighton's many haunted hotels and pubs – which really merit a whole book to themselves. The strange stories concerning Preston Manor and the séances conducted there in the 1890s and the ghosts associated with the nearby Preston old church are covered in Chapter Five. Chapter Six ranges over a variety of haunted locations, correcting the error of those who think ghosts are invariably linked to ancient buildings.

As well as revisiting some relatively well known hauntings, I am also pleased to include a number of hitherto unpublished or obscure cases, including some gathered by the Society for

Psychical Research. The oldest stories in this book date from the last quarter of the nineteenth century whilst the most recent experiences were collected early in 2006. In the process I have attempted to relate the facts to some of the many theories about ghosts. It is thus hoped that knowledge can be built upon knowledge and that further research will be encouraged.

However, anything approaching rational assessment is complicated by an apparent myth-making tendency in human beings when faced with inexplicable events. Having no ready explanation for the causes of psychic phenomena it seems that the imagination readily works overtime to fill the yawning gaps. Thus, famous characters from Brighton's history such as the Prince Regent and his lover Mrs Fitzherbert are grafted on to otherwise anonymous ghostly manifestations at Brighton Pavilion and elsewhere, whilst noises in pub cellars are attributed to phantom smugglers rather than the shades of toiling bar staff from years gone by. Similarly, the famous actress Sarah Bernhardt is linked to a grey lady at Brighton's Theatre Royal although there is no plausible reason why she should appear here rather than in the many other theatres at which she performed in life. Perhaps with the spread of the gaudy minimalism of the global village the urge to celebrate the romantic past is an inevitable and local necessity.

For my own part, I have no doubt that ghosts are a real phenomena and that the existing boundaries of scientific knowledge will have to be considerably enlarged to explain them. The question of *what* ghosts exactly are or represent remains a mystery and I think no single explanation or theory can adequately cover all the reported phenomena.

The author of a popular ghost book treads a difficult path. On the one side there is the desire of a large audience who love traditional ghost stories and want to be entertained. On the other side there is the intense interest of a smaller but no less demanding audience who want to know the truth about psychic phenomena and are looking for answers to ultimate questions about human existence. I hope that this book will manage to bring at least some small measure of satisfaction to both sets of readers (who often overlap) and also please both visitors and local people alike.

ONE

THE HAUNTED LANES

For generations the world famous Lanes at the heart of Brighton have enjoyed a lively reputation for being haunted. Their image as a centre for psychic activity was first fostered by writers of popular ghost books and then successfully maintained by the guides for the ghost walks and tours which pass through the area today.

If one man can be held responsible for promoting the phantom-laden reputation that the Lanes enjoy, it is undoubtedly the writer and ghost hunter Robert Thurston Hopkins (1880-1958). Hopkins tirelessly championed the paranormal side of the Lanes in the last decades of his life, seeing them as an almost spectral manifestation in themselves. Of them he wrote, 'In this Lilliput village, full of the oddest relics of dwellings, drowsy little shops and cul-de-sacs, time seems to have stood still, and it is easy to see that it is a place of considerable antiquity, and appropriately the gathering-ground of all manner of phantoms and inexplicables'. Many shops and buildings in and around the Lanes have been the scene of unexplained incidents over the years, including apparitions, strange noises, poltergeist phenomena and even a haunting smell of exotic flowers reported in a curio shop in Meeting House Lane during the 1950s.

Regrettably, it seems Thurston Hopkins was prepared to deliberately weave wholly invented material into supposedly genuine accounts of ghosts in the interests of telling a good story. Indeed, he rather gave the game away in *Ghosts Over England* (1953), where he admitted that many of his stories might not be factually true. There is little that can be said in his mitigation, other than to note the peculiar effect that stories of ghosts and the supernatural can have in stimulating the powers of the human imagination.

Nonetheless, when it came to Brighton and the Lanes, Thurston Hopkins does seem to have been more respectful of truth – or at least folklore – than on other occasions, although a fragmentary tale of a phantom finger writing on the ceiling of one shop may well be a poetic whimsy. However, the need for greater accuracy with Brighton stories was driven by a strong element of personal necessity. As the founder of the respected Society of Sussex Downsmen, Thurston Hopkins had a local reputation to protect and he would have risked immediate exposure by members of his local community had he been willing to pass off invented stories whilst using their names. Furthermore, there exist a number of reports of ghostly activity which are quite independent of Thurston Hopkins' colourful story telling and which indicate that the reputation of the Lanes for being haunted is well deserved.

The Lanes, Brighton, c. 1960.

The screaming skull in the Lanes

Undoubtedly, the strangest ghost story associated with the Lanes is that of the screaming skull allegedly heard by a thirteen year old boy at the end of December 1953.

Along with Halloween, newspapers and magazines invariably pick the Christmas season for reporting ghost stories, since tales of spectres provide a perfect traditional balance to the holly and red-faced laughter. But as 1953 drew to a close, the national press noted a marked decline in ghost reports. Such was the deficit of sightings that the President of the Folklore Society, the eighty-five-year-old historian Margaret Murray, took the opportunity to declare: 'Our ghost population is now a shade of its former self. There is nothing like the numbers of them that there were in my younger days. Maybe it's because of better street lighting. They always show up better in the dark you know'.

The now defunct *Reynolds News* took up the challenge of discovering ghost sightings that Christmas, publishing its nationwide results on 27 December 1953. Most extraordinary of all the crop of ghost reports received was the claim that on Boxing Day an ancient skull exposed in an antique shop in the Lanes had been heard to scream, terrifying a thirteen year old boy. The sound was described as 'a fearful yelp'!

From the information it had hastily been able to gather, the *Reynolds News* reported, 'The skull which has been grinning malevolently in the window … for several years, was originally

*Robert Thurston Hopkins with the
screaming skull.*

found in the thick wall of an old farmhouse at Rushlake Green, Sussex'. What the *Reynolds News* did not divulge was the full history of the grim relic which had been on display in the shop since 1945. How exactly the skull came to lie in a Brighton antique shop is confused, as the history of the skull was one of successive relocations, sales and intermittent burials throughout the twentieth century. But it seems that the skull was none other than one of the celebrated 'Screaming Skulls of Warbleton Priory', an ancient building standing some miles from Brighton. Unknown to *Reynolds News* numerous tales of ghostly activity were associated with the skull long before it had arrived on the premises.

The skull had first received national publicity nearly fifty years earlier, in an article published in *Notes and Queries* in 1905. Originally, the skull was said to be a protective talisman for the lands attached to Warbleton Priory. The ancient farmhouse stood on the site of an Augustinian Priory and the skull had been preserved in the building for well over a century. Its origins were suitably mysterious, with different tales being told of its provenance. One claimed the skull was of a murderer who killed a past owner of the Priory. Presumably, the assassin was executed for his crime and denied a Christian burial, or the victim's relatives revenged themselves upon him and kept his skull as a trophy for descendants of the victim. What were purportedly the bloodstains from the crime were still being shown to curious visitors at the Priory at the beginning of the twentieth century. In later versions, there were two skulls kept at the Priory which were supposed to be the remains of a pair of monks who had quarrelled and killed each other, whilst in yet another variant, R. Thurston Hopkins maintained that one of the skulls was a mummified head discovered by a workman in the wall of Warbleton Priory Farm around 1820. As it was removed an enormous toad was said to have scuttled from the hole. The farmer took it back inside and kept it on a beam in the roof. Over the years the tissue and skin on the head rotted down leaving only the bare skull. In this more presentable condition it was placed upon the family Bible in the front room.

All traditions agreed that if ever the skulls were removed from the house they would scream or cause unpleasant manifestations until they returned. One of the heads was said to have been buried in consecrated ground but it mysteriously exhumed itself and was found the next morning on the doorstep. Another tale told of a departing tenant who attempted to take a skull with him when the farm changed hands. His rash decision caused 'strange noises and inexplicable happenings' both at Warbleton Priory and at his new home. Windows rattled, doors banged shut by themselves and horses displayed signs of terror at an unseen presence. The man swiftly returned the skull to the Priory, whereupon manifestations ceased.

Unfortunately, after the publicity in *Notes and Queries,* the precise whereabouts of the skull or skulls in the first half of the twentieth century becomes less clear. Thurston Hopkins claimed that he visited the Priory in 1905 only to learn it had disappeared. But some eighteen years later, in 1923, Hopkins saw a Warbleton Priory skull for sale in a Brighton antique shop. However, he declined to buy it remembering the legend and fearing the consequences. He later claimed to have revisited the Priory around 1930. The then occupiers denied all knowledge as to the whereabouts of the skull and its ghostly traditions. But as he left, a farm labourer allegedly told him that a pair of skulls had been securely walled up in the building, behind two carved stone heads from the Priory.

It is at this point the story seems to have become garbled, with a companion skull being moved for some unspecified purpose to a farm at nearby Dallington. The source of this rumour is Hopkins, who claimed the farmer at Dallington had told him that an enormous wind had blown up to thwart attempts at burying it. However, in 1945 Hopkins then claimed to have seen the skull exposed again for sale in a different shop in the Lanes. Recognising it as the same skull he had seen in 1923 – his memory for craniums must have been good – he made enquires with the owner. He was told that strange banging and thumping sounds had been heard in the shop ever since the arrival of the skull. This story of manifestations in the antique shop was also collected by Stephen V. Ziegler, the author of a pamphlet on Warbleton Priory. He learned that on the first night of ownership the antiques dealer had left the skull in the shop. The following morning neighbours complained of strange noises emanating from the premises. The same occurred on the two following nights, aggravating more people. By now very concerned, the dealer placed the skull in an outhouse, whereupon the noises ceased.

Again Hopkins did not buy the skull. However, the haunting cannot have proved too traumatic since the same skull was still on display some eight years later and with an eye for a publicity opportunity Hopkins arranged to be photographed examining it as an illustration for his book *Ghosts Over England,* published in 1953. It was this skull which then allegedly went on to scream on Boxing Day. Nonetheless, it was not immediately removed, if later, more reliable accounts of the skull are accepted.

Sometime afterwards – perhaps as a result of the publicity in December 1953 – the skulls were purchased by the owner of Warbleton Priory, a Mr Peter Dunn, and returned to the building. For unknown reasons, one was offered up for sale in *The Times* in 1963 at a price of ten guineas but it appears no buyer was forthcoming. One account of the ultimate fate of the supposed screaming skulls was gleaned from local enquiries by veteran ghost hunter Peter Underwood, at Rushlake in Sussex in 1971. The skull or skulls had apparently gone missing from the Priory during the Second World War (this might be consistent with one of them showing up in the Lanes in

Above: *Warbleton Priory*

Right: *The screaming skull hidden in an alcove at Warbleton Priory, c. 1974. The cranium has been removed.*

1945) and returned in the 1950s. Thereafter, the story circulated that the skulls had been interred permanently, with Peter Underwood being told they had been given what was described as a 'decent burial' about five years previously. However, Stephen Ziegler's guide book *Warbleton Priory* reveals that they were concealed within the building and rediscovered in renovation in 1973. In the late 1970s, the ghost hunter Andrew Green obtained a photograph of one of the skulls in its hiding place, the top of the cranium now missing. They have been preserved in the building ever since.

Certainly, the traditions – real or concocted – concerning the skulls mirror legends at many other locations in Great Britain. Most share common features of guardianship of property and a reputation for causing sinister paranormal happenings if ever removed. The protective element hints at pre-Christian roots, but it seems more probable that many were either Catholic relics or examples of the Tudor, Elizabethan and Jacobean fashion for memento mori, the skulls acting as poignant reminders of the mortality of man. Over the years their purpose was forgotten and legends grew up around them. The most likely origin for the Warbleton Priory skulls is from monastic burials on the site.

As with other screaming skulls, the evidence for manifestations in the Lanes arising from the Warbleton skull never gets much beyond hearsay and rumour. However, one cannot discount the possibility that superstitious dread surrounding such objects might generate psychological stress for those possessing or handling them. If so, the unconscious mind might create powerful hallucinations or even generate genuine poltergeist effects which would be ascribed to the malevolent powers of the skull.

The Grey Nun

The most famous ghost of the Lanes is undoubtedly the Grey Nun. It seems certain that Thurston Hopkins did not invent the story of the phantom nun in grey who flits through the Lanes at twilight. One route takes her from Brighton Place to a bricked-up doorway in Meeting House Lane; another along the narrow twitten between the Black Lion and Cricketer's Inn. A rare and infrequent ghost in the open, she was first reported by a woman firewatcher during the Second World War. According to Leslie Robinson in his book *The Lanes of Brighton* a nun-like figure was seen by a woman firewatcher during the Second World War. It was late at night and the fire watcher was surprised to see what appeared to be a woman in a grey hooded robe walking alone along Meeting House Lane.

She called out to the figure and, receiving no reply, decided to follow her. The figure glided silently through a bricked-up doorway in Meeting House Lane and vanished. The story has an air of plausibility; the best state of mind for seeing a ghost appears to be a relaxed one when thinking of nothing in particular (certainly not consciously thinking of ghosts – as many a ghost hunter will admit!), and many sightings occur between midnight and dawn. During long nights fire-watching a person might well find their mind idling, and it was perhaps in this receptive state the Grey Nun was briefly glimpsed.

The bricked-up doorway is still visible in Meeting House Lane and is often pointed out on ghost tours. Over the years a number of people have complained of uneasy feelings when standing close to it. Auto-suggestion may well play a part but many have been happy to attribute this to the presence of the Grey Nun. Other accounts claim that she wanders the Alleys at twilight, 'until someone notices that in the dark cavity of her hood there is no face.'

Right: *The Grey Nun.*

Below: *The twittern down which the Grey Nun glides.*

The bricked-up doorway where the nun has been seen to vanish in Meeting House Lane.

The legend of the Grey Nun is a gruesome one. She is said to have been a young novice attached to the Priory at Lewes which had connections with the Chapel and Priory of St Bartholomew, built in 1120, and destroyed by the French attack on Brightlingshelme in 1514. Because of the dangers posed by robbers and raiders, a detachment of soldiers were lodged as guards at the Priory on one occasion. The nun fell in love with one of the soldiers and the couple eloped. Unfortunately, they were swiftly overtaken, captured and brought back to the Priory for punishment. The soldier was summarily tried and executed as a deserter, whilst the hapless nun was walled up alive and left to starve to death. Legend avers that this barbaric punishment was inflicted upon the young woman because the hypocritical religious community believed it sinful to shed human blood.

Perhaps unsurprisingly, there is no historical evidence to support this story and little evidence that nuns were ever attached to St Bartholomew's Priory. Furthermore, although such stories are told in many parts of Britain, there is no convincing evidence beyond tradition that walling-up alive was ever imposed as a punishment in monastic establishments. It is certainly the case that during the medieval period nuns were sometimes walled up in small cells, but this was at their own request in ferocious demonstrations of religious zeal and extreme self-denial. Once bricked up the voluntary penitent would be regularly fed and ministered to through a small hatch, but otherwise lived in total hermit-like seclusion from the rest of their community. It is possible that such legends arose from garbled accounts of these voluntary incarcerations and that after the Reformation the discovery of such walled-up cells (and possibly the bones of those who had expired buried within them) fuelled the legends of bricked-up nuns.

The difficulties of ascribing the figure to the return of an anonymous medieval nun are overcome if another interesting possibility is considered. This is that the ghost is a comparatively recent apparition from the nineteenth century of a former pupil of the Emigrant House Charity School which was established at Brighton Place in the nineteenth century. The uniform of the female pupils included a head scarf which might have been perceived as the cowl of a nun. Children from the school sailed to Australia on 11 December 1886. Tragically, the ship sank at the end of January 1887; nearly all the female passengers on board were drowned. Another alternative theory is that the figure is simply the apparition of a Brighton fisherwoman from the eighteenth or nineteenth century with a head covering.

If either of these theories is correct, then it would appear that the name the 'Grey Nun' has simply been a convenient and romantic label to attach to any hooded female apparition witnessed in and around the Lanes. Furthermore, given the size of the area she is said to prowl, one wonders if she might also be connected with the far more frequently reported 'Grey Lady' of the Theatre Royal or the White Lady of the Dome, not far away?

The phantom monk

As well as the Grey Nun the Lanes can also claim a ghostly monk, supposedly a former brother from St Bartholomew's Priory. Like many monastic phantoms he is anonymous and lacks any legend to explain his presence. He is said to frequent the area around the town hall and particularly the cellars beneath shops in the Lanes. On at least one occasion he also seems to have appeared above ground, at John Beal's, a stationer's shop which stood in the Lanes for many years.

The witness was a Miss Fermor, who was working late in the stockrooms with the manageress, a Miss Goodbody, in the December of 1951-52, sorting out a stock of diaries for the new year. Miss Goodbody went down into the shop to collect a list. Shortly afterwards Miss Fermor thought she heard footsteps ascending the stairs, but more quickly than those she would associate with the manageress. According to Joan Foreman, who interviewed Miss Fermor for her book *The Haunted South* (1978), she called out, 'Is that you Goody?' casually assuming that it was the manageress as there was no-one else there in the evening. Getting no reply she turned and found herself gazing at a phantom monk in dark robes standing in the room with her. One might have said that she was face-to-face with the monk but for the disturbing detail that there was no head within the hood, only darkness. Horrified, Miss Fermor fled the stock room and ran downstairs. Finding the manageress sitting at a desk she poured out details of her disturbing experience. Not surprisingly, neither woman worked late at the shop again for a long time.

This seeming shyness of apparitions about displaying clear facial detail is a recurring feature in stories in Brighton and elsewhere. It also raises the possibility that the Grey Nun and the monk may be one and the same figure.

Phantoms of the Town Hall

The ghostly monk is also said to wander Brighton Town Hall. However, a far better known spectre is the ghost of a former Chief Constable of Brighton, the only Chief Constable in British police history to have been murdered on duty. The reputation for the town hall being haunted may have begun with the fact that it was constructed over a burial ground. When the foundations for the town hall and market were being dug in the nineteenth century a number of complete skeletons, together with assorted skulls and bones, were discovered. However, the

The town hall, scene of a Chief Constable's murder.

incident for which the town hall became truly notorious was the murder of Chief Constable Henry Solomon, which occurred on 13 March 1844 when the building was also being used as the town's first police station.

His killer was a local man, John Lawrence, aged twenty-three, who had been arrested along with another man for the theft of a carpet from a shop. On being taken into custody, Lawrence appeared highly agitated when questioned by Solomon and was moved to a warmer room in the basement where there was a fire burning in the grate. However, Lawrence became even more agitated and suddenly seized up an iron poker and struck Henry Solomon across the head. The blow proved fatal and Lawrence stood trial for murder at the Lewes Assizes. Following conviction he was hanged outside Horsham Jail.

Council employees based at the town hall have had strange experiences in the building over many years, including sightings of Henry Solomon. As a result the basement was never used until its conversion into a small police museum in July 2005. Long serving staff also recall the strange reactions to the cellar of Fred, the town hall cat, who was employed on the council payroll in the 1980s. Although Fred would roam freely about the building he always refused to enter the basement. Fred died about twenty years ago and is buried in the animal cemetery in Preston Manor Park. His reactions provide an apparent confirmation of the folkloric belief that cats are 'psychic barometers'. The behaviour of Fred brings to mind experiments at a haunted house in Kentucky by a parapsychologist, the late Robert Morris, in the 1970s, who found that a cat was among a number of animals showing adverse reactions to a room in which a murder had been committed.

With such a background, it is perhaps not surprising that in 1982 Brighton Borough Council was prepared to take on ghost hunter Andrew Green (1927-2004) to investigate cases of hauntings in properties owned by the council. Popular ghost walks also commence from outside the town hall on the first Saturday of every month.

The Meeting House

Dating from 1805, the Friends' Meeting House in Meeting House Lane has had a reputation for being haunted by an unseen presence and phantom footsteps for over thirty years, during which time it has been used as an education centre. In December 1974, authoress Elizabeth Ing of Hove told a reporter for the *Brighton and Hove Gazette* that she had felt a ghost in the Meeting House when she had first come to Brighton, and that she sensed her presence every time she visited the building. She was not all frightened by the experience having, she claimed, much experience of ghosts ever since she was a child. Elizabeth Ing believed that the presence was the Grey Nun.

A more disturbing experience was shared by two women attending an evening class in April 1997, who were accidentally locked in the building after visiting the ground floor toilets and were unable to find a way out. Fortunately, they had mobile telephones and were able to summon assistance but not before they shared the unnerving experience of hearing footsteps and a key being turned in a door inside the empty building. Fortunately, following a call to a friend who contacted the police, the key-holder was eventually found and the two women were able to make a thankful exit from the building.

Haunted pubs in the Lanes

The Lanes can also claim a share of Brighton's many haunted pubs and inns, notably the Black Lion, the Druid's Head and the Cricketer's Inn. Although in January 2006 staff at the Bath Arms in Meeting House Lane maintained that strange noises heard recently in the pub were attributable to underground tunnels this explanation may not extend to phenomena reported in at least three other taverns.

Phantom martyr at the Black Lion

On the wall of the Black Lion pub in Black Lion Lane is a memorial plaque to Deryck Carver, the first Protestant Martyr burned at Lewes in July 1555. The plaque was designed by the artist Eric Gill in 1926 and was originally set in the wall of the old Black Lion Brewery that stood next door to the Black Lion Inn. Although considered the second oldest building in Brighton the Brewery was demolished in 1974 and replaced by the dour office block which now occupies much of the site. Part of the cellars still survive under the Black Lion and it is these which are reputed to be haunted by Carver's ghost.

In life, Deryck Carver was originally a Flemish immigrant who established the brewery in 1546 and lived and worked on the site, which also encompassed what is now the Black Lion pub and the nearby Cricketer's. Carver used his premises for organising Protestant meetings and worship during the reign of Queen Mary, contrary to the teaching of the Church of Rome and

The Lanes.

The plaque to Deryck Carver burned at Lewes in 1555.

Deryck Carver's house.

in defiance of the law enacted to suppress Protestant worship. It was during one of these secret gatherings in October 1554 that Carver was arrested by an armed party of men led by Sheriff Edward Gage of Firle. Carver was taken in chains to London and imprisoned in the infamous Newgate Gaol for eight months. In June 1555 he was taken with a fellow Protestant named Lauder before Bishop Bonner of London for questioning. Both men openly confessed they were Protestants and stoutly refused to abandon their faith, Lauder declaring, 'I will never go from these answers as long as I live'. Deryck Carver agreed.

On the tenth of June Deryck was again asked if he would repudiate his faith. He rejected the authority of the Pope's offer of conversion, stating in words guaranteed to provoke his inquisitors '....for your doctrine is poison and sorcery. If Christ were here you would put him to a worse death than he was put to before.' On the question of papal authority he derisively observed, 'You say you can make a man a god: ye can make a pudding as well.' Faced with such recalcitrance, the Church authorities decided to make an example of Carver and he was taken to Lewes for public execution and burned alive in the centre of town on 22 July 1555.

Witnesses at his execution were impressed by his piety and stood in awe at his relaxed demeanour. Deryck calmly undressed and climbed into the barrel in which he was to be burned, his Bible also being thrown in with him. He prayed for the Lord not to forsake his wife and children and for his own forgiveness. Despite Carver's death, brewing continued on the site and by the end of the 1940s it was an established local tradition that his ghost haunted the cellars of the brewery as an anniversary ghost. According to details recorded by the *Brighton Argus* on 26 March 1968, a long-serving foreman at the brewery confirmed that 'on certain evenings in July unexplained noises have been heard in the vaults.' Local journalist Peter Dally wondered 'Could

The Black Lion.

they be the restless spirit of Deryck Carver disturbed by the apparent indifference and neglect of a nation which benefits from his beer?' but the foreman refused to be drawn further on either the nature of the sounds or their possible cause. At the time it was hoped that conservationists would save the building in order that both it and Deryck's ghost could become one of the heritage attractions of Brighton, on the grounds that, 'This unique mixture of blood and beer history would help to balance the somewhat ostentatious splendour of the Royal Pavilion and its associations with a corpulent fun-loving prince.' Unfortunately, efforts to save the building failed.

No manifestations have been reported in the cellars of the office block (now a bank administrative building) but phenomena have been reported in the two nearby pubs. The current licensee of the Black Lion inn mentions that staff have experienced a cold and eerie atmosphere in a part of the cellar since 2004 and complained of 'a feeling as though a dead body is there'. In the 1980s there were reports of poltergeist phenomena and the unexplained movement of beer barrels in the cellar, and a shadowy figure was reputedly seen by a builder working in an upstairs room in 1995.

The Cricketer's inn.

The Cricketers pub

Next door to the Black Lion stands the Cricketers which also shares a long-standing reputation for being haunted. The Grey Nun is said to flit along the narrow passageway between the two buildings but undoubtedly the better attested phenomena have been reported inside the Cricketers itself, though without the marked sense of a presence reported in the Black Lion. Although the current licensees state that they have had no manifestations in the last few years, it was certainly a different state of affairs between 1993-96, when poltergeist phenomena and unexplained footsteps were reported in the building. Glasses were moved and beer taps turned off, matching events at a great many other haunted pubs both in and around Brighton and elsewhere in the UK. Incidents include moving or breaking glasses or ashtrays, tampering with beer taps and barrels, the touching of bar staff and curious sounds. So typical is this pattern of phenomena within licensed premises that it would not be excessive to speak of there being a 'haunted pub syndrome'. According to local writer John Rackham a ghost of a man was also seen on occasion in the pub.

Certainly, the Cricketers pub has attracted interesting personalities over the years – everyone from Graham Greene, author of *Brighton Rock*, to Roslyn D'Onston, one of the controversial suspects for the identity of the infamous Whitechapel serial murderer Jack the Ripper.

The Druid's Head pub.

The Druid's Head

For sheer duration, the most haunted pub in Brighton must undoubtedly be the Druid's Head in Market Street. This popular tavern can claim stories of a haunting stretching back ninety years, and despite extensive refurbishment it maintains some of the ambience of a much older building. Although a flagstone in the bar carries the date 1510 there is much doubt as to the real age of the building and when the licence was first obtained, probably in the mid-nineteenth century.

The evocative name of the pub is derived from its proximity to the former site of a supposed stone circle which antiquarians of earlier times were prone to ascribe to the Druids, the sacred priesthood of the Celts. Stories abound of smugglers and secret tunnels at the pub whose history is uncertain. Two blocked-up entrances in the cellar encouraged belief in the Druid's Head having been a base for smuggling operations. They are said to be the former entrances to secret tunnels used to convey contraband and cheat the revenue men. One is said to run to the Fish Market and the beach and the other to the Pavilion (in another version, the tunnel is said to run beneath Brighton Place and the Sussex Hotel). The passages were supposed to have been revealed during renovation during the 1960s. One wonders if smugglers would really have gone to the expense of constructing lengthy passages when bribing night watchmen or excise officials might have been a simpler and cheaper alternative. Whatever the case, it would suggest that the liquor trade – in one form or another – has been associated with the Druid's Head for a long time.

Although even more colourful stories have the Prince Regent surreptitiously using the tunnels to obtain contraband or for meeting lovers, it seems more than possible – alas for tradition! – that

The haunted cellar steps in the Druid's Head.

the bricked-up places in the cellar are simply closed off alcoves or chambers once used for storing barrels or bottles. Nonetheless, echoes and occasional collapses in subterranean chambers and tunnels might account for unusual noises in the premises above over so many years.

The earliest stories are accounts of phantom footsteps reported at the pub during the First World War, along with a rumbling sound. Folklore ascribes this to a smuggler who became trapped inside one of the tunnels and perished, or even one who was walled up alive! According to R. Thurston Hopkins these noises in the cellar always ceased when the wife of landlord called down asking the ghost to desist. It always obliged, earning the ghost the nickname 'the Polite Spook'.

Between 1945 and 1975 the pub was run by a landlord named Les Walker, who was said to have been 'quite convinced' of the haunting. In the early 1950s he told R. Thurston Hopkins that his daughter complained of 'funny men' coming up to the attic room where she slept. Later reports stated that Les Walker had supposedly seen the ghost and heard strange noises, along with all three of his daughters. Research into the Druid's Head by ghost hunter Andrew Green in the 1970s indicated that these reports may have been exaggerated, although one daughter had heard her name being called. In 1978 Andrew Green interviewed a Mrs Susan Funnell (as she had then become) about her time at the Druid's Head.

Susan Funnell recalled that about twelve years before she had been awoken late one night by her name being called. Her sister, sharing the same bedroom, also heard the voice, but their other sister in the next room heard nothing. 'It wasn't a joke,' Susan stated, 'it really happened, but I never saw anything and I am very doubtful now about the place being haunted.' Nonetheless, some thirty years of monitoring reports at the Druid's Head led Andrew Green to believe that genuine phenomena occurred inside the pub, including poltergeist-style movements of bottles and glasses, lights switching themselves on and off and occasional apparitions.

Andrew Green advanced the theory that ghosts represented a currently mysterious but natural phenomena involving electromagnetic energy. He did not believe that manifestations provided evidence for the existence of spirits or life after death; rather, that they represented a form of electromagnetic energy which continued after the death of the person who had produced it, and which could be picked up by sensitive people or on sensitive measuring instruments.

*Tunnel entrance in
the Druid's Head.*

Derek Woods, who took over the licence in 1975, believed he had seen the apparition for himself, but just for a 'fleeting instant'. He stated, 'It was just a hooded figure that flitted under the stairway in the main bar and I really couldn't say what it was. It was about 11.30 at night, shortly before Christmas. We had closed up and were just going to bed.' It would be tempting to immediately label this apparition as a monk or nun, given the pub's position near the end of the Lanes. However, it would equally be consistent with a person seeking to conceal his identity, perhaps one of the smugglers from years gone by.

Equally, it might also be the apparition of an unknown female, a lady dressed in red who crosses the bar past the same stairway. She was seen by a barmaid named Cindy Wilkinson in August 1994, standing next to a customer (who was unable to see the figure). The sighting came after strange knocks were heard earlier in the previous year by a relief manager Simon Woodhall. In May 1993 he had been alone in the lounge (the pub being shut) when he heard unexplained knocking on the wall with the kitchen. He rushed into the kitchen only to find it empty.

Customers have also glimpsed apparitions. A psychically sensitive member of the Ghost Club, Mr Lionel Gibson, visited the pub in the mid-1990s. In the back of the public bar he felt sensations of a presence and 'out of the corner of my eye glimpsed more than once a tall dark figure, wearing a heavy coat and hat, which only later I thought incongruous on a warm summer afternoon. Every time I turned my head there was nobody there.' This was before Lionel Gibson learned of any ghost stories attached to the Druid's Head.

In January 2006 the current licensee and bar staff confirmed that strange noises continued to be heard coming from the cellar during the night. The sounds were so loud that they could be heard upstairs. A growing number of ghost hunting groups are also expressing an interest in spending a night in the building. In the event of any repetition of manifestations it will be interesting to see if the ghost is still prepared to stop on request!

TWO

HAUNTED BRIGHTON HOMES

Over the years many houses in and around Brighton have been the scene of hauntings and poltergeist activity. Houses which seem warm and welcoming in daytime can take on a different atmosphere at night, perhaps linked with chemical changes in the brain during the hours of darkness which may stimulate greater psychic receptivity. The following are a selection of cases involving local homes spread over more than a century.

The Prestonville Road haunting

What was for seven years the most haunted house in Brighton stood in Prestonville Road, off Dyke Road. Not only are the strange events at this house among the best documented but the haunting represents, as Dr Alan Gauld, a former president of the Society for Psychical Research, described it, '…one of the eerier cases of which we have records'.

The haunting was initially investigated by one of the founders of the Society, Edmund Gurney (1847-1888). It was also to be the last case Gurney investigated, for he was to die at the Royal Albion Hotel in Brighton some ten days later in strange circumstances which have proved a source of controversy and suspicion in the years since (see the Royal Albion Hotel, Chapter Four). Edmund Gurney was at the forefront of efforts by the Society to collect testimony on hauntings and apparitions. A sensitive and kindly man, he seems to have had an ability to connect with witnesses. Gurney came to Brighton on the 13 June 1888 to talk with Mrs Clara Gilby, the widow of an army officer, who had been driven out of her home in Prestonville Road by ghostly phenomena.

Mrs Gilby's first experience had occurred within a fortnight of moving into the house in November 1887 when she was awoken one night by what she described as 'a deep sob and moan.' Her first thought was that it was one of her children and she immediately got up to check them in the bedroom, which was at the back of her own room. Both children were sleeping soundly. On returning to her room she was then disturbed by another sob and 'a thump of

Above: *Prestonville Road.*

Left: *Edmund Gurney.*

Opposite: *Prestonville Road today.*

somebody or something very heavy'. But what was to follow was even more alarming: 'I sat in up in bed, looked all round the room, then to my horror a voice (and a very sweet one) said, 'Oh do forgive me!'. The voice came again and again, three times in all.

Naturally alarmed, Mrs Gilby left her room and woke the maid. Further sounds followed including more sobs and noises 'like heavy boxes of plate being thrown about'. The maid suggested she should

ring a large bell but Mrs Gilby did not want to wake the neighbourhood. The noises eventually ceased with a 'low moan' in the morning.

The sounds turned out to be only the opening shots of the ghost in a campaign of disturbances which led Mrs Gilby to record details of the haunting in a diary and eventually drove the family from the house. As well as voices, apparitions were witnessed including a phantom of a small woman, a pale female face seen peeping around a door, two other faces, strange lights and a shadow. But equal alarm seems to have been generated by other uncanny noises and the continuing sense of an invisible presence either trying to get into house or actually on the loose inside it. The doorbell would ring mysteriously when no person was physically present outside, but far more disturbing were the knocks upon inner doors and the sight of handles being turned or rattled as though someone was urgently trying to get in. Sometimes doors would mysteriously open and shut.

Mysterious footsteps, bangs and rumbles as though furniture was being moved around were heard whilst other sounds were more subtle, such a curious sound like paper being screwed up or thrown around (this may have been the same sound identified by later visitors as the rustling of a dress). Ghostly music, including the sounds of a musical box and single notes played upon a piano, was also heard.

By March 1888 the disturbances had became so bad that Mrs Gilby and her children fled the property. The financial loss and inconvenience in leaving the property early were as nothing to freeing themselves from the haunting. Of Mrs Gilby, Gurney wrote, 'She struck me as an excellent witness. I have never received an account in which the words and manner of telling were less suggestive of exaggeration or superstition.'

Gurney's investigation was cut short by with his tragic death in Brighton 10 days later. In the interim the case was taken up by Frank Podmore, a rather sceptical member of the Society. Podmore established that following the departure of the Gilby family the house had been occupied between the 23 and 28 May 1888 by four men intent on an experiment in ghost hunting. They claimed various experiences, including the appearance of a misty vapour, but their rather credulous belief in all things supernatural led to their testimony being given little value. But Podmore found it more difficult to dismiss the testimony of an earlier occupant who had been traced. This was a Miss Morris who had lived in the house with her family between October 1882 and December 1886 and who confirmed the hunter's tales.

The Morris family experienced a number of phenomena, including the same mysterious doorbell ringing that occurred during Mrs Gilby's tenancy and on one occasion the apparition of a woman with a pale sad face was seen. Miss Morris took a robust attitude to the phenomena and on one occasion searched the house armed with a poker, suspecting that a burglar had gained entry!

In August 1888, G.A. Smith, the mentalist whom Gurney had investigated, moved into the house with his new wife. During the next thirteen months between August 1888 and September 1889, thirty-nine different people stayed overnight in the house, a number of whom reported strange noises. During his tenancy Smith kept a diary recording the continuing tricks and disturbances of the invisible presence which give a real feel as to what it is to occupy a badly haunted house:

> December 9th … I was in the house alone, writing at my desk. Time 8.30. Suddenly I heard a noise which seemed to come from the hall, outside my room door. I can only compare the sound to that which would be made if half a brick were tied to a piece of string and jerked about the linoleum – as one might jerk a reel to make a kitten playful…

Smith carried out an immediate search of the corridor with a reading lamp but could find no explanation for the noises. He returned to his desk only to have the sounds resume five minutes later. This time he pursued them in the dark, groping his way to the kitchen where he turned up the gas lamp but found nothing untoward.

The attraction of the ghost to music also continued, with notes being picked out on a guitar in the house in the summer of 1889 but no more apparitions were seen. What is to be made of Smith's testimony? It should be noted that years later Smith was accused by a self-confessed fraudster of cheating in telepathy tests which Gurney had organised (Smith denied the allegations). Interestingly, Smith remained a member of the Society for Psychical Research until his death in 1961, which suggests he had a genuine and long standing interest in psychic phenomena. Even removing the testimony of Smith we have the evidence of two separate households prior to his occupancy. The phenomena at the Prestonville Road house ceased in September 1889 and when the Society enquired further it was informed it was still quiet in March 1890.

The haunting was attributed to the suicide of a woman in the house prior to the occupancy of the Morris family. In their own way these phenomena illustrate a number of features which are typical of haunted properties in Brighton. The case like many others seems to have been a mixture of a haunting and poltergeist noises, suggesting there may be an interaction between certain people and particular places.

Interestingly, a later report of manifestations at a flat in Prestonville Road some fifty years later was recorded by the ghost researcher Frank Usher. At the end of the Second World War a lady named Anne Johnson, a former Mayoress of Hove and wife of the Mayor of Brighton between 1960-61, moved into a flat in Prestonville Road. She often felt someone sitting on her bed although the room was otherwise empty. When she left the house she made further enquiries and learned that many years earlier a man had killed his wife in the same room. Regrettably, at this distance, it is unlikely the flat can be firmly identified but there is obviously a suspicion it could have been in the same house occupied by the Gilbys in 1888.

Margaret Verrall.

The little old lady at Vernon Terrace

Some ten years after the Prestonville Road investigation the Society for Psychical Research published the experiences in Brighton of a lady who was destined to become one of its distinguished women members, the classics scholar Margaret Verrall (1859-1916).

As a young woman Margaret lived at No. 24 Vernon Terrace in Brighton. Early one evening in September 1879 she had been washing her hands in a little room at the end of a passage leading to the front door when she heard footsteps. Looking up she saw what she described as 'a little old lady' coming towards her. She was dressed in a dark dress gathered in full folds around the waist, a grey knitted shawl over her shoulders fastened with a brooch and wearing a cap. But although she seemed to be walking towards her, she could not distinguish any face.

Margaret took the figure at once to be a hallucination but was neither startled nor alarmed. She watched as the figure continued coming towards her, vanishing before reaching the room she was in. Over the next few weeks she saw the figure of the old lady on at least three occasions, always walking towards her. Once it appeared when she was sitting with her sister (who was unable to see it). Her calm observation enabled her to note further details; that a brooch fastening the shawl was like a circular brooch with a hole in the centre once worn by her great-grandmother, a Mrs Watkins who had died ten years previously. Yet on no occasion was the old lady's face visible only, 'a blank within the cap' (it says much for her detachment she was not disturbed by this). Otherwise the figure seemed life-like and to fit in perfectly with its surroundings

Margaret described her experiences without a trace of sensationalism. She freely admitted it that it seemed to be hallucinatory in nature, stating '...that although at the time I saw the figure I had no reason to suppose I was not well, I had had a short illness in Switzerland.' Why the effects of this illness – if it was a factor at all – should have manifested as the apparition of an old lady remained a mystery.

In mid-October Margaret returned to Cambridge to resume her studies and where she was ultimately to spend the rest of her adult life, marrying Arthur Verrall, professor of classics at Trinity College, in 1882 and later enjoying her own successful career as a classicist at Newnham College. By her own admission, she did not think about her experiences at Vernon Terrace in Brighton and would perhaps have forgotten them entirely but for a strange incident that occurred in the Cambridge house in which she was living.

She recalled that '…one evening, as I was going upstairs to my room, I heard footsteps coming along the passage at the top of the house, and looking to the left (instead of turning to the right to my room) to see who it was, saw my old lady coming towards me. There was no-one else in the passage; the gas was lighted and I saw the figure plainly.'

Margaret maintained her calm approach, apparently unperturbed that the ghost had seemingly followed her from Brighton. As on the first occasion she had heard footsteps, these being the only times there were accompanying sounds. But the experience proved to be the last manifestation of the figure which never appeared again.

But perhaps the apparition of the old lady takes on a greater significance when the subsequent life and career of Margaret Verrall are considered. For Margaret Verrall went on to become active in psychical research and in the last fifteen years of her life became involved with a celebrated set of mediumistic communications, 'the cross-correspondences'. After her marriage, she also befriended Frederic Myers, who was a neighbour and one of the founders of the Society for Psychical Research and author of *Human Personality* and became very interested in psychical research and attended gatherings with leading mediums at Myers' home. It was no doubt Myers who encouraged her to record her experience with the apparition and inspired by these associations she decided to cultivate her own psychic gifts.

After Myers died in 1901 Margaret took up automatic writing, a psychic skill in which a medium produces written messages whilst in a trance state. Margaret Verrall excelled at automatic writing. Unlike most mediums she did not need to go into a light sleep to produce scripts, only a state of relaxation. Furthermore, the messages she produced were not short or banal like many mediumistic utterances, but involved hundreds of cryptic and complicated messages in English, Latin, Greek and French, some of which seemed to predict future events. Her daughter Helen also took up automatic writing in 1903. When the material from both women was later compared with messages produced by other mediums in Britain and abroad, researchers noted certain similarities between the different scripts, suggesting that discarnate intelligences – possibly including Frederic Myers himself – were trying to communicate their survival by way of a complex code. These communications became known as the 'cross-correspondences' and constitute some of the most remarkable evidence for mediumship obtained in the twentieth century.

Scholars have continued to analyse and debate the meaning of these and other cross–correspondences material in the years since, a number maintaining that they constitute strong evidence for survival after death. But few recall that perhaps the first sign of Margaret Verrall's psychic gifts came in the form of the apparition she had experienced in her home at Brighton.

The mysterious girl at Lansdowne Place

If mystery surrounded the causes of the phenomena at Prestonville Road and Vernon Terrace, perhaps an even greater mystery lay behind both the life and identity of the pathetic girl who became the haunting presence at Lansdowne Place following her death in 1899. The story came

Lansdowne Place in 1908.

to light due to the testimony of a Miss L.V. Stevens who was engaged as a domestic maid at the house in Lansdowne Place in June 1902. Miss Stevens seems to have been a thoughtful and intelligent woman who provided a detailed account to the Society for Psychical Research, of her own experiences and the story connected with them. The house at the time was owned by an elderly lady, Miss Bell, who also employed a cook and took in lodgers. Miss Bell seems to have been a considerate and benign employer, but she initially concealed the truth about Miss Stevens's predecessor as maid.

At first Miss Stevens noticed nothing untoward in the house, other than that the cook, a Miss Margaret Hilton, would often stay up very late talking with her in the kitchen. Miss Stevens formed the impression that the cook was in some way reluctant to go upstairs by herself after dark and would find almost any excuse to avoid doing so. Indeed, Margaret would often sleep down in the kitchen rather than retire to her own room.

Nothing untoward happened to Miss Stevens in her first six months as a maid in the house. But early one December morning, as she was dressing by candlelight with the door slightly open, she saw a figure pass in the corridor outside. It returned and suddenly put its head round the door, peeping into her room. Miss Stevens stated: 'It was dressed in black with long black hair and over all a gauze veil through which features were not distinctly seen.'

Miss Stevens was not at all frightened by the figure or its brief intrusion, thinking that in general appearance it was not unlike Miss Bell. Indeed, she suspected that it might be her employer or Margaret playing a joke. On going downstairs she found them together in the kitchen and charged them with playing tricks. However, both denied it and Miss Stevens noticed the strange passing expressions between the cook and her employer. But as her experience had been in no way alarming she thought nothing further of the incident until, shortly afterwards, a lodger in the house reported seeing a strange female figure walking up the stairs. He had initially thought that this was Miss Bell going upstairs for a bath until he discovered that she had, in fact, been downstairs suffering from illness.

As with the apparition at Vernon Terrace, facial features of the ghost were obscured.

It was then that the story behind the phantom came out. Some three years earlier, in 1899, Miss Bell had taken in a poor teenage girl as a domestic servant. Despite having no references the girl begged to be given a trial period, promising to be honest and faithful. Miss Bell was a tender-hearted woman and moved by the girl's pleas agreed to engage her. All was well for two weeks; then the girl was taken seriously ill. She said that she had no family or friends and that there was no-one to be communicated with about her. Together with Margaret Hilton Miss Bell decided to nurse the girl back to health but it was to no avail. Her condition seriously worsened and within a week the girl was dead.

Shortly before the end, Miss Bell tried to give some comfort to the dying girl and lent over to kiss her. However, the girl became agitated at her gesture and tried to pull away, crying piteously, 'No, no, you mustn't kiss me, you wouldn't want to if you knew all!' But still she would say nothing about herself or the reasons for her strange outburst. She died without revealing the troubling secret on her conscience.

Following the girl's death, Miss Bell contacted the police, hoping to identify the girl and discover if she had been linked with any crime, scandal or misfortune. But her efforts were in vain. Nothing was ever discovered about either the background of the girl or who she really was. To the little stock of money which she left, Miss Bell added some of her own to prevent the girl from being buried in a pauper's grave but her real identity remained a mystery.

Soon afterwards the ghost of the girl began to be seen in the house. Miss Bell was the first to see the figure, some two or three months after the sad death of the girl. She continued to appear at intervals, mainly in the early part of the month and often on the eighth of the month (according to the story Miss Stevens heard, the girl had died on the eighth). The ghost was never seen in the lower part of the house but always between the bathroom and top storey or in the top storey itself. Margaret Hilton had seen the ghost and this explained her reluctance to go upstairs alone at night. Furthermore, Margaret was sleeping in the room in which the girl had died and on one occasion she had awoken to see the girl standing at the foot of her bed.

Several lodgers in the house also saw the figure and others felt it push against them on the stair. Miss Stevens was also to see the ghost herself again, '.....in an exactly similar way to the first occasion, peeping round the door into my room in the early morning'. Miss Stevens left the house in September 1904 for good. Miss Bell continued to live in the house until her death sometime before 1908 but whether the ghostly girl was seen again remains unknown.

It is interesting to note that the facial features of the apparition which Miss Stevens saw were partially concealed, a pattern which occurs with a number of other ghosts reported in Brighton and at other places in the UK. It almost seems that having concealed her identity in life the girl wished to continue to remain anonymous after death.

The sinister foreign man at Marine Parade

Around 1890 rumours spread in Brighton that a Dutch (or possibly German) man living at Marine Parade named Anherst had been murdered during a quarrel arising from a card game and his body hidden. There was nothing to substantiate these claims although the stories were widespread. It seems quite possible that Mr Anherst had merely decamped abroad – perhaps to escape gambling debts – and settled in another home on the Continent, never to return. Undeterred by any tales about the house, an eccentric retired military man named General Warner took the property as a Brighton home and lived there with his servants, off and on, for well over a decade, apparently without any problems,.

In 1909 the house was taken on a lease by a rather flamboyant widow Mrs Wentworth and her three cats, at a rent of £60 per year. Mrs Wentworth initially occupied the house alone but planned to take lodgers and guests both for financial reasons and for company. On 20 October 1909 she experienced what she described as an 'uncanny sensation' in the large house. Certainly, the place was one which provided much food for the imagination. It had large cellars which suggested that at one time it had been an inn and there were stories – so common throughout central Brighton – of there having been tunnels from the house to the beach which were used by smugglers.

Very soon she became convinced that the house was haunted by an unseen presence. She felt strange sensations, heard footsteps and doors banging and witnessed strange reactions from her favourite cat Cheetah who seem to spit and react to an invisible presence. Mrs Wentworth decided to turn ghost hunter in her home and planned to sleep in each room in turn and await manifestations.

Having started with a level-headed approach – and Mrs Wentworth appears to have sensibly recorded dates and events – her investigation undoubtedly became coloured by spiritualist beliefs. In a lengthy account, Mrs Wentworth freely admitted being a devout and enthusiastic spiritualist, counting mediums among her personal friends. She also held regular séances in the house, twice a week. It was therefore inevitable she would enlist their help.

A special séance involving nine 'level-headed, sensible men and women' was duly organised with the medium being a Mrs Fielding who had moved to Brighton from Sheffield. The séance began with prayers and organ music and soon afterwards Mrs Fielding underwent a dramatic vision of a 'dreadfully cruel-looking dark man like a foreigner', standing near the door. The figure held a knife upraised as if about to strike somebody, and she heard a woman's voice cry out: 'No – No! Not that! Not that!' before the spectre vanished.

Marine Parade today.

At a subsequent séance another medium, a certain Madame Adine Ratcliff, claimed to have seen looking round the door '…a most terrible looking dark foreign man about forty or forty-five', whose face was 'simply diabolical' and who was seen brandishing an upraised carving knife. Madame Ratcliff maintained she entered into a trance condition and psychically followed the sinister knife-wielding man around the house. He led her first upstairs to the best bedroom and pointed at the bed and then turned and led her to the cellar.

A third medium, a Madame Alexandra Campbell, was then invited to stay in the property, occupying the best bedroom to see what would happen. Madame Campbell did not claim any ability to see spirits, only to hear them, a faculty termed 'clairaudience'. During the night she heard a fight taking place. The fighting spirits struggled all over the room and at last the attacking one threw his victim on the bed. Madame Campbell felt their weight fall on to her, and one spirit form gripped her round the waist. Highly alarmed she cried out 'In the name of God, I bid you – Go!' and the sensations ceased. She looked at the time to find it was 1.30 in the morning. Madame Campbell was so distressed that she declined to stay in the house any longer and returned only for meals. For the rest of her stay in Brighton she rented a room away from the house in Marine Parade.

Thereafter, Mrs Wentworth decided she would conduct an experiment with the main bedroom by offering it to a prospective employee, a Miss Josephine Johnson, but without telling her of its reputation. Miss Johnson was described as a level-headed young woman of thirty-four years who was interested in serving in the house. However, her terrifying experiences in the bedroom soon changed her mind, proving equally as traumatic as those of Madame Campbell.

It seems that Miss Johnson's experiences commenced on the first night she slept in the room. Mrs Wentworth noticed Miss Johnson came down to breakfast the next morning looking white and drawn and it took little to draw her story from her. Miss Johnson revealed that during the night she had awoken to see the ghost of a terrible-looking dark man at her bedside and seemed to hear the sound of a struggle. Then the frightening spectre lent over and seized her by the throat as though to strangle her and she could feel the pressure of hands on her throat. A curious aspect was her also sensing the presence of Mrs Wentworth in the room, although she had not physically left her own bedroom (Mrs Wentworth took this latter detail as indicating she had been present in spirit form protecting Miss Johnson).

Still maintaining that she knew nothing about ghosts in the room Mrs Wentworth somehow persuaded Miss Johnson to sleep in the room again. On the second night she was again disturbed by a spectral vision but this time, only a hand alone, 'a great big horrible man's hand came right up in front of my face.' Badly shaken, Miss Johnson left immediately to return to her family home in Rotherhithe as her health appeared to have deteriorated after just two nights in the house. Interestingly, her experiences had also occurred just after 1 a.m. and Mrs Wentworth learned that she subsequently had to receive medical treatment. Soon afterwards, Mrs Wentworth was threatened with legal action by Miss Johnson's father, for having placed his daughter in 'the dreadful room'. This was a threat he was still making in the first few months of 1910.

By this stage Mrs Wentworth was also having problems with the alarm which was developing among the servants whom she had employed in the house, who also believed they had witnessed manifestations. A maid named Ellen Pentecost had seen a swarthy-looking man in a black cloak walk through the closed door of the haunted bedroom, which had by now become known as 'The Ghost Room', as Mrs Wentworth breathlessly recorded in a typed account she composed in January 1910. The room was duly sealed on account of its by now grim reputation. A manservant named Ernest Bennett had also felt 'something' pulling at his foot as he lay in bed one night in the room opposite, which caused him to kick out and then dive under the bed covers.(One cannot help thinking this presence was one of Mrs Wentworth's three pet cats.)

Mr Bennett also contributed to the growing atmosphere of excitement and hysteria by suggesting that a slight depression in the cellar and some loose bricks might indicate a grave site. The influence of such speculations can be seen in Mrs Wentworth's increasingly dramatic description of her premises, recording that the coal cellar '…is a weird terrifying place, and is perfectly dark' and of her wine cellar, '… a veritable catacombs in miniature.' She added, 'We all wonder if poor Mr Anherst was murdered and buried there, and the truth hushed up. I want to pull up this place & see if bones or a body are to be found there.'

Fortunately, a medium counselled against this (perhaps thinking matters were spiralling out of control) and instead recommended that Mrs Wentworth contacted the Society for Psychical Research and give them an account of the experiences. It was also perhaps the threat of legal action from Miss Johnson's father which encouraged her to seek help from the Society.

A thoroughly sober investigation was duly carried out by the intriguingly named Mr Wortley Baggally from the Society. An experienced investigator who had conducted sittings with the famous Italian medium Eusapia Palladino, Baggally brought a sceptical view to events. As he confided to his notes, he discovered nothing to support the ghost of the dark, foreign-looking man loose in the house.

Regarding Mrs Wentworth, he found her a rather impressionable woman who suffered from hearing problems and probably could not distinguish the sounds she claimed to have experienced in the house. Baggally considered – perhaps somewhat charitably – that rumours and stories about the house had stimulated the imaginations of both the household and its spiritualist-inclined visitors. In his view, the experiences had arisen through auto-suggestion, with stories passing from one impressionable person to another, resulting in hysterical reactions, hallucinations and nightmares, particularly as regarded the unfortunate Miss Johnson in 'The Ghost Room'. It is interesting to see from Baggally's notes that as soon as he became involved with the case, the ghost mysteriously ceased its activities.

Having interviewed the witnesses, Mr Baggally decided to complete his investigation by spending two nights in the haunted bedroom himself and risk an encounter with the strangling man. He wrote: 'I gave the alleged ghost the best conditions to enable him to make an appearance, viz, I put out the lights and kept the door of the room unlocked, but he did not condescend to pay me a visit.' He added laconically, 'I heard no noises'.

Calm returned to the household. All plans for excavating the shallow dip in the cellar floor were quashed. Perhaps the events had brought a degree of drama and excitement into the retired life of Mrs Wentworth in Brighton as well as providing a self-serving confirmation of her beliefs. Nearly a century on, it is impossible to reach a final conclusion as to the events at Marine Parade. Nonetheless, an interesting detail appears in Baggally's notes from his interview with Ellen Pentecost, the maid. He learned that some twenty-two years before her grandmother had been employed in the house as a servant. During that time her grandmother had reported strange noises and had seen a ghost on one occasion. It transpired that the house in Marine Parade had indeed long been said to be haunted – but by a woman.

The poltergeist at Kings Road

Few ghostly disturbances are ever as dramatic as those claimed at Marine Parade. By far the most common manifestations reported to psychic researchers are mild forms of poltergeist phenomena. Poltergeists have been known for centuries and a growing number of such incidents were reported in and around Brighton as the twentieth century drew on. One which possessed a number of unusual features was reported to the Society for Psychical Research in 1948. A Mrs Priestley living in Kings Mansions along Kings Road, Brighton contacted researchers with details of strange events at her home over the previous four years.

Events had begun in March 1944 when a bright light was seen in a bedroom in the middle of a black-out. Two years later a bed was disturbed and cushions were thrown about. Mrs Priestly also suffered a blow to the face for which there was no apparent explanation. Sheets and pillows were again disturbed the following year and a person leaving the property encountered a physical force and felt themselves being pushed back inside.

Perhaps the strangest aspect of the case was that anomalous voices were heard over the telephone, a relatively early example of what was later termed electronic voice phenomena (EVP), most commonly associated with anomalous voices supposedly recorded on tape. However, in contrast to alleged EVP phenomena where the voices can be very difficult to hear, these were immediately heard, although they uttered baffling messages. On 2 September 1947 the voice on the telephone said, 'Wait till October 5th' but nothing occurred on the date. In January 1948 a voice said 'Mind how you go' but again the message lacked any discernible significance. Whether the voices were wholly hallucinatory or misperceptions of interference on the line or the work of a hoaxer was not determined.

Unfortunately, further enquiries elicited no more information, the Research Officer having suggested that objects could be ringed with chalk to see if any movement might be detected. No further reports came from the house and it may be that like so many others, the poltergeist – if that is what it was – faded away, never to return. However, the case was to set a pattern for later poltergeist outbreaks in a number of Brighton homes just over twenty years later which eventually led to Brighton City Council appointing its own ghost expert to deal with problems in council homes.

The beating heart at Hampton Terrace

One of the most curious of all Brighton ghost stories took place on the night of 1 February 1961. It is an extraordinary story reminiscent of the Edgar Allan Poe story *The Tell Tale Heart*. But this was no fictional invention but an account of strange sounds heard coming from the room of a house at Hampton Terrace where an eighty-eight year old man lay dying.

The old man was attended in his final hours by his wife and his daughter, Mrs Harvey, who was a successful music teacher. Both women had been in a long vigil by the bedside. About 10 p.m., the attending physician, a Dr Leekham, who had been ministering to the comatose patient advised that his life was drawing to a close and that there was no more that could be done. As the doctor left he advised both mother and daughter to take some much needed rest.

In an account supplied by Mrs Harvey to researchers, she stated that her mother retired to her room and soon fell asleep. Mrs Harvey remained up and shortly afterwards became aware of a noise like an amplified heart beat coming from her father's room. Mrs Harvey wrote '…there was a distinct pattern of sound … regular for so many beats and then long gaps before resuming again'. Mrs Harvey listened for what she estimated as about an hour to the strange noise before waking her mother. Both women were greatly alarmed at hearing the sounds which continued for around four hours. 'We could not summon enough courage to go into my father's room again until 7 a.m. when he had gone...'

Both Mrs Harvey and her mother were encouraged in the belief that the sounds were paranormal by the opinion of Dr Leekham to whom they first related the experience. He considered that the noises were in some way supernatural. He confirmed that in his terminal condition her father's heartbeats would be feeble but the sounds matched the rhythm of the heart of the dying man.

A report was compiled by an experienced investigator, Mr Ackerman of the Society for Psychical Research who at one time had also looked into the alleged haunting of Borley Rectory in Essex, dubbed 'the most haunted house in England' and also considered by Guy Lambert who served as the Society's secretary. Lambert was a keen proponent and champion of what is known as the 'geophysical explanation' for hauntings and poltergeist phenomena. Lambert maintained the theory that many cases of noises and object movements in haunted houses were actually being caused by vibrations set up by flows of underground water or high tides. With Brighton being by the sea, it might seem a natural epicentre for disturbances. As Hampton Terrace was some distance from the sea, Lambert considered that water running down through drains from the direction of the Devil's Dyke, an Iron Age earthwork near Brighton, might be the culprit. (In local folklore the Dyke was said to have been built by Satan in an attempt to flood local churches centuries ago). Lambert theorised that an overflow of rainwater from a downpour on Devil's Dyke had set up a rhythmical sound in the local drains and sewers. It was this thumping sound which had been heard by Mrs Harvey and her mother. Inspection of the area revealed that running water could be heard flowing in a drain situated near the property.

Both Ackerman and Mrs Harvey seem to have been minded to accept the explanation proffered by Lambert, although Mrs Harvey was still forced to declare 'What a coincidence!' to the fact that the sounds should occur exactly when her father was dying. Nonetheless, in August 1963 Lambert declared that as far as the Society was concerned the case was closed.

There are reasons for finding Lambert's theory less than satisfactory as an explanation. The duration of the sounds over a period of hours is definitely unusual but it does occur in one or two other Brighton stories. Although most serious ghost researchers would not wholly dismiss Lambert's ideas as a possible cause, there has been little evidence to substantiate his theory in the decades since.

Devil's Dyke. Was a flow of water to Hampton Terrace responsible for the strange phenomena there in 1961?

More recently, his geophysical theory has resurfaced in a new form, suggesting that it may be electromagnetic discharges from underground rocks and fluctuations in the earth's magnetic field which may act on the temporal lobes in the brains of sensitive individuals and trigger hallucinations. Furthermore, Ackerman's own notes suggest that Mrs Harvey may have possessed mediumistic powers herself. Unfortunately, we do not know on what basis the investigator reached this intriguing conclusion. But given that poltergeist disturbances are often linked with stress, it raises the possibility that she may have caused or created the noises using latent psychic powers from her own subconscious at the time of her father's passing. Certainly, strange knockings occurring at the time of death are known from folklore from Britain and Ireland. A further curious detail emerges from the notes on the case in that Mrs Harvey also mentioned that the room had a reputation for being haunted prior to February 1961. Couples living in the property as lodgers had reported strange sensations in the room and two husbands had awakened in fright in a 'cold sweat and hair standing up', feeling a presence. Unfortunately, this aspect of the case was never pursued.

The house at Down Terrace

In July 1970 Alfred Knight and his family applied to Brighton Council to re-house them because of manifestations of a terrifying presence at their home in Down Terrace. A great many ghost experiences occur in bedrooms (around a third of collected sightings seem to have occurred when the witness was in bed) and this initially seemed to be the case with Down Terrace. Mr Knight awoke about 3 a.m. to feel someone, or something, crawling over him and shaking the bedpost as though to get him out of bed. He thought at first it was his three children but they were all asleep. It transpired that Mrs Catherine Knight had suffered similar experiences for two years but had not told her husband. She had also experienced the sensation of someone or something touching her hair, again at 3 a.m. in the morning. Although the children did not see anything they were reluctant to go upstairs at night and frequently woke up screaming. The couple also recalled that on the first night in the premises they had heard unexplained footsteps on the stairs.

There were concerns for the health of the family and Mr Knight was considering changing jobs so he could be at home during the evening. The family considered moving even though they had chosen the house because of its proximity to a hospital where the older of their two sons was receiving sun-ray treatment three times a week.

The *Evening Argus* newspaper appears to have been struck by the plight of the family (fortunately the bed-shaking occurred too early to be branded as an alien abduction). In a then unique move, the Knights contacted the Citizens' Advice Bureau seeking re-housing. Fortunately, the council were open-minded though Brighton's deputy housing manager stated 'I have never heard anything like it before. I've been in housing a good many years now but this is the first case of a council house being haunted that I have heard of.' In fact, it was to the first of a number of reports of haunted council properties in Brighton over the next twenty years, some of which made national news.

The proliferation of cases led Brighton Council in 1982 to appoint the ghost expert the late Andrew Green as a consultant on haunted properties. Throughout his life Andrew Green took a very rational approach to ghostly phenomena, always looking for normal explanations and in many cases succeeding in finding them. But in a number of cases Green was convinced that the only plausible explanation lay in the existence of psychic phenomena.

The haunted vicarage

During the nineteenth century and early twentieth a great many ghost stories were set in dwellings occupied by the clergy. Writing of poltergeists, the famous psychical researcher Harry Price remarked '…they can hardly keep away from rectories…they love the homes of holy men.' However, the mid-twentieth century onwards showed a marked reduction in the number of haunted clergy homes. One exception to this decline – for which a number of different causes might be postulated – was the now demolished St Martin's Vicarage in Upper Wellington Road Brighton in which a case of 'haunting smells' was recorded.

According to the story, which made both the local press and the pages of the *News of the World* in 1972 under the heading 'The vicar gets a spook cook', the unexplained smell of baking bread was experienced coming from the cellar. The vicar's wife Mrs Lesley Baden stated 'I have woken in the middle of the night and smelled lovely meals cooking and bread baking. At first I thought it must be just the smells of my own cooking.' In another interview with the Brighton *Evening Argus* mention was made of the 'mouth-watering fragrance of superb meals' in the house.

However, an accumulation of incidents had convinced the family an invisible presence was in the house. When they had first moved in four years previously the vicar the Revd Peter Baden had initially sensed someone upstairs but had attributed noises to the joists settling. Their domestic help Mrs Celia Knight had also been alarmed by hearing footsteps and by upstairs doors suddenly opening and closing on a calm day. According to information obtained from parishioners the vicarage had a reputation for being haunted. Refreshingly, the household responded to their unseen presence with a positive attitude with the children finding 'it all a bit of a joke', which seems the perfect attitude to take to a harmless haunting.

Ventnor Villas

A month after story of the haunted vicarage the Brighton *Evening Argus* reported a more disturbing case of another family far less happy about their persistent ghost. 'It defies the vicar; opens bolted doors and moves with the family' began the article in the *Evening Argus* which appeared on 10 March 1972. 'It' was a ghost which Mr Peter Arnold and his family believed was following them wherever they went in Brighton, from home to home. Mrs and Mrs Arnold and their two sons had moved four times but each time manifestations had followed them, including two properties in Ventnor Villas.

Events had begun when the family were living in a four-roomed basement at Tisbury Road in Hove. Mr Arnold had seen the apparition of a little girl dressed in Victorian costume standing in the room holding a doll. His wife Josephine laughed at his claim but her humour evaporated when a cupboard fell inexplicably upon her in the kitchen. She was certain it had been pushed. Heavy footsteps were also heard coming from an empty room above the flat and a strange luminous mist appeared.

The ghost was blamed for other problems with doors and cabinets which the couple found would not stay shut. A carpenter was employed to fix one but it repeatedly came open. In the end he abandoned attempts to fix it. The couple moved to another flat in Ventnor Villas only to have the phenomena follow them. Again they experienced problems with a cabinet refusing to stay shut. A cabinet repeatedly opened even though bolted at the top with a key turned in the lock. A Christmas tree started shaking without explanation. The vibrations grew so strong that the floor was showered with pine needles. Even after they had been swept up and thrown away a trail of pine needles was discovered stretching across the floor between the kitchen and the lounge.

A vicar attended the flat and said prayers but with no discernible effect. He told the family that there was a presence but that it was not evil. The family also received alternative guidance

Opposite: *Ventnor Villas in the early twentieth century.*

Right: *Andrew Green.*

and counselling including suggestions that Mr Arnold himself was psychic. Once the tensions in the family had been expressed and released the phenomena appear to have ceased.

Private house at Gladstone Road, Hove

During many years of investigation into Sussex ghosts, expert Andrew Green frequently visited private homes where the residents believed themselves to be haunted. Often he found fears had been compounded by thoughtless spiritualists, amateur exorcists and self-proclaimed witches who declared evil spirits were loose. Many psychics might be well-meaning but others were attention-seeking cranks and fraudsters who by accident or design played upon the vulnerabilities of households.

On 22 July 1978 Andrew Green investigated phenomena at a council house in Gladstone Road, Hove which had been the home of a married couple and their two children for ten months. The couple had been glad to move into the property having been on the housing list for eight years. However, they were being disturbed by raps and taps, particularly on windows. Sometimes the sounds resembled someone walking up and down or approaching a door and then walking away. Shuffling sounds were also heard, and previously in March, the young son had been scared by a flash of light. It happened again and by Sunday night the boy refused to sleep in the room. Other happenings included the lounge door opening by itself, a scent bottle moving mysteriously and an incense-like smell.

Like many poltergeist cases, there was disturbance of the bedclothes. Blankets were found tucked in differently from the way they had been laid out. The baby's pram in the hall was moved from by the door and found parked halfway along the hall. Perhaps the most disturbing of all was finding that a baby had seemingly been turned around in its cot, the infant being found lying long ways but otherwise completely unharmed. Feelings of an 'icy cold' were also experienced; these seemed particularly intense in the bedroom.

The household had previously been visited by a Baptist exorcist and a medium who proclaimed that the spirit of a woman named Alice was present in the house. According to the medium, Alice had 'died of a broken heart' in an upstairs room in the property. Regarding those phenomena which could not be explained, Andrew Green's diagnosis was that the events were being triggered by stress within the household rather than a spirit. Once genuine manifestations had been witnessed there had also been a tendency to credit unusual but normal happenings with a paranormal significance. The nearby railway and traffic could have caused noise and vibration and had perhaps been responsible for some of the strange sounds.

A similar case arose at a house in Elm Terrace, Hove in 1985. The efforts of various psychics and an exorcism failed to end the disturbances, leading Canon Dominic Walker, an adviser to the Church of England on psychic matters, to sensibly propose that the problems were likely to be of a poltergeist nature linked with stress.

With such cases the solution is often to bring about a change in lifestyle; the removal of stress often proves the key to ending the phenomena.

The strange lights of Shirley Street

At the end of 2002 and in early 2003 there were reports of strange lights haunting Shirley Street in Hove and stories of a strange patch of light at a house in nearby Clarendon Street. Some attributed them to ghosts whilst others drew parallels with UFO phenomena. By January 2003 the *Evening Argus* was reporting that people were becoming 'accustomed to the daily apparitions of Xs and bars which flicker along their street'. In January 2003 what purported to be a photograph was also produced, showing what some considered to be an alien–like figure. Taken by a local woman who refused to be named, and reproduced in local newspapers, it was suggestive of a tall thin figure apparently wearing a spherical helmet. The woman stated 'I am absolutely petrified of them [the lights] because I cannot explain how they get there or what they mean. I don't know if they are a sign from the aliens or a warning that something is about to happen.' However, as with many alleged ghost photographs, interpretation of the light markings in Shirley Street as a humanoid figure or even as some kind of manifestation were very much in the eye of the beholder. Certainly in recent years there has been a remarkable growth in the number of claimed photographs of alleged apparitions. There are now probably more photographs being claimed than at any period since the late Victorian era and it is worth recalling the words of the celebrated nineteenth-century medium Stainton Moses, 'Some people would recognise anything [as a ghost]. A broom and a sheet are quite enough for some wild enthusiasts who go with the figure in their eye and see what they wish to see ... I have had pictures that might be anything in this or any other world sent to me and gravely claimed as recognised portraits'

A further objection to a paranormal explanation for many similar orbs is that the air is constantly filled with minute specks of moisture, smoke or dust and these may be recorded on sensitive cameras, particularly where the flash is situated close to the lens, as with most modern cameras. Also there are far more electromagnetic discharges in different forms into the environment than ever before and many of these can contribute to anomalous images which turn up on photographs. Nonetheless, some photographs showing fogging and misting effects may indicate the presence of anomalous electromagnetic energy of some kind.

As to the lights in Shirley Street no single explanation has yet conclusively accounted for all the sightings. Doubtless publicity may have fuelled claims but may also have increased the number of genuine witnesses coming forward. Atmospheric effects, the misperception of natural and man-made sources of illumination and wishful thinking may all play a part. However, anomalous light phenomena have also been observed in other parts of Sussex and indeed across much of the UK, particularly in the winter months. As a county Sussex has many well-attested stories of strange luminous spheres and will-o'-the-wisp-like apparitions, spread over more than a century. As a result the possibility of something genuinely mysterious having taken place in the area cannot be discounted.

THREE

SPECTRES OF THE DOME, PAVILION AND THEATRE ROYAL

Dubbed the 'greatest folly of them all' the Pavilion and Dome have been the best-known architectural features of Brighton for the best part of two centuries. As a world famous attraction and potent local symbol the buildings both receive many thousands of visitors each year. However, few sight-seers ever seem to encounter ghosts or complain of being troubled by strange experiences during their visits. The atmosphere of these grand bijou palaces seems relentlessly sunlit and the presence of large holiday crowds rarely favours sightings of apparitions. But for many years there have been stories of hauntings at the Pavilion and Dome including claims that the ghosts of George IV and Martha Gunn, the famous Brighton bathing queen, walk both buildings.

More recent accounts tell of other ghostly phenomena experienced from the 1970s onwards, though attempts to penetrate the mystery by successive researchers have seldom been as fruitful as they would wish. Officials at the Pavilion and Dome have as often as not been hesitant to discuss these experiences which seem to be confined to a small number of staff who remain working in the building after it has closed for the day and visitors walking the grounds late in the evening.

The story of the construction of the Pavilion began in 1783 with the coming of age of the Prince George Augustus Frederick, later King George IV. Born in 1762, the Prince was as a young man considered handsome, gallant and charming. But on reaching the age of 21 his immediate reaction was to hasten down to Brighton to visit his scandalous uncle, the Duke of Cumberland, who occupied Grove House, close to the site of what is now the Royal Albion Hotel (now under the north wing of the current Pavilion) and set about enjoying himself. The Prince took a liking to Brighton and in the following year he decided to establish his own household in the town. It was to be the beginning of a life of over-indulgence, both in terms of his personal life and in the grandiose architectural construction that is his most striking monument.

His building of a home in Brighton was justified on the basis it was convenient for bathing in the sea. In reality, it was to maintain a lair for what became his three main interests: eating,

The Pavilion today.

horses and love affairs. Construction began in 1784, by which time he had fallen in love with a Brighton widow, Mrs Maria Fitzherbert, who was twenty-five years of age and lived nearby. There is no doubt that the reputation of Mrs Fitzherbert suffered from her connection with the Prince, whose boisterous friends could often be a public nuisance. On occasion at night, Mrs Fitzherbert had to endure impromptu serenades from drunken members of the aristocracy who would deliberately beat a path to her door in the knowledge of her involvement with the Regent.

Stories that the Prince built a tunnel under the building to connect the building to Mrs Fitzherbert's home are untrue; another fanciful tale had the Prince constructing a tunnel running as far as the Druid's Head in order to meet his lovers. But a tunnel was built between the Pavilion and the Dome, in addition to the extensive wine cellars, to facilitate access by his Highness. The purpose of this appears to have been two-fold. The subterranean link provided a dry route between the Pavilion and the stables in bad weather and in later years it helped conceal from popular gaze the growing obesity of the Prince.

Enormous sums of money were soon applied to the building of the Pavilion, and the Prince even became unpopular with his own father George III on account of his profligacy. By 1786 George III was forced to approach Parliament for £161 000 to be added to the civil list, much of it to cover the Prince's debts. When on 2 August 1786 an assassination attempt by a mad woman upon the monarch failed, King George nonetheless refused to see his son who had hastened to Windsor to enquire after his father's condition and express his congratulations on his survival of the attack. However, no serious effort was made at any point to halt the construction of the Pavilion or stem its rising costs.

Initially the Pavilion was known as Brighton House but from 1800 onwards it underwent a series of extensions and elaborate decorations. The eighteenth-century Age of Reason was coming to an end and the ruling classes were exhibiting a passion for all things Chinese which shaped the development of the building. In turn this was superseded by an enthusiasm for Indian styles, an influence which manifested particularly in the design of the Dome as a stable block. A

The Pavilion in 1784.

combination of architects and designers finally created the Pavilion and Dome of today, so that the resulting 'domes and spires suggest that it was mislaid by the Slave of the Lamp in a careless moment'. It is, however, infinitely more charming than twentieth-century efforts at imposing architecture such as the Millennium Dome.

In 1805 the Prince obtained an order from the Lewes Court to enclose the old road through the site but under the condition, 'That should the Prince at any time cease to require the use of the same proposed to be given by the inhabitants, or should the Pavilion and grounds at any time pass from his occupancy or be sold, then and in either of the said cases the said portion was to revert to the use of the inhabitants.' This clause was to play an important part in ensuring that the Pavilion was later saved for the town nearly fifty years later.

Although his self-indulgence had become legendary, the Prince was also known for his generosity, on occasion throwing large free banquets for the poor of Brighton and hosting other popular social events. But his accession to the throne as King George IV in 1821 meant that the Prince had fewer opportunities to indulge himself and others in Brighton and he died seven years later in 1828, by which time his visits had become infrequent compared with the roistering days of the past. The direct links with royalty were severed completely within a few decades when Queen Victoria decided to dispose of the buildings, reputedly because of the 'ill-bred populace' of Brighton who even 'poked their noses under her bonnet'. Eventually the building was acquired by the Brighton Corporation for £53,000 and has been in public ownership ever since.

It is a long-standing Brighton tradition that the ghost of George IV walks the tunnel between the Pavilion and Dome, but only one sighting is ever believed to have occurred and details of this are sparse. In any event, the identification of the ghost as George VI may be questioned for, as Joan Foreman observed in her book *Haunted Royal Homes* (1987), one figure in Regency costume may appear very much like another. She also applied this philosophy to the story of the phantom of Martha Gunn who was friendly with the Prince and allegedly appears in the kitchens. It seems that, in the absence of any other details as to the identity of a haunting presence, the inevitable temptation for folklore is to pick the most famous historical or romantic character known to have a connection with a site.

Statue of the Prince Regent.

Between the two World Wars the ghost of Martha Gunn was reportedly seen by a friend of a local man, Mr James Martin. It was Mr Martin who in turn supplied details to R. Thurston Hopkins for his book *Ghosts Over England* (1953). According to the story, the man was employed in organising catering arrangements for a large banquet organised at the Pavilion one night. The tables had been fully prepared and the witness was engaged in making some minor adjustments to a floral decoration, when something prompted him to look up from his work. He saw a dark, roundish figure which he thought was an elderly female appear from the kitchen and pass by the tables. The figure seemed particularly determined to reach the top table. The caterer tried to approach the figure but it seemed to have the ability to evade him, keeping a considerable distance away no matter how close he tried to approach. Finally, the shape then vanished through an adjacent door. The caterer rushed to the door and went into the corridor only to find it completely deserted. He then hurried to the end of the passage and enquired of the attendant whether he had seen an old lady go past. The attendant had seen nothing.

In the course of making further enquiries about the apparition, the caterer later examined a file kept at the Pavilion of old clippings, portraits and prints, hoping to find a picture which showed a resemblance to the figure he had seen. According to the account given by the witness, the form had worn a long, 'bunchy' skirt, a triangular shawl and an old fashioned bonnet and he felt it bore a marked similarity to a picture in the album of Martha Gunn, a friend of the Prince Regent and famous in her life as 'the Brighton Bather'. Martha Gunn died at Brighton on 2 May 1815 at the age of eighty-eight. Whilst this identification may not be the most the reliable, the story has a degree of plausibility for other reasons. The ability of apparitions to avoid observers who attempt to catch them has been noted in other cases in the literature of psychical research and is a small detail which adds credence to the account.

The Royal Pavilion as reconstructed in 1817-20.

A presence on the stairs

In January 1975 reports reached the Society for Psychical Research of further manifestations at the Pavilion, including an apparition in period costume seen by a security guard around 1973. Apparently fearing ridicule he kept quiet about the experience for two years. He also stated that a member of staff had suffered an unexplained push whilst descending a staircase. Rumour had it that a murder had once been committed on the staircase though neither the identity of victim or the perpetrator were known in the oral tradition. When other staff had complained of being pushed on the same stairs an additional rail was fixed to give support.

Two experienced investigators for the Society decided to look into the stories of the haunting in the mid-1970s. These were the late Manfred Cassirer and his wife Pauline who had first picked up stories on an informal visit. However, the management of the Pavilion at the time proved less than enthusiastic about enquiries. Following an exchange of letters, including the rejection of a proposal to hold a vigil in the building, they agreed to meet with Cassirers and discuss the experiences of Pavilion staff. Accordingly, Manfred and Pauline Cassirer visited the Pavilion again on Wednesday 29 January 1975 and were given conflicting stories. A Mr Legget informed them that another member of staff, a Mr Butler, had undergone 'experiences' and confirmed the story of the member of staff pushed down the stairs. However, when meeting Mr Butler they found him reluctant to answer questions and he would not provide the name of the security guard who had seen the apparition. He poured cold water on the stories of ghosts and attributed them to the warped sense of humour of a security guard who was fond of making up tales. However, when they asked further questions about his own experiences he denied having any encountered anything at all in the five years he had been at the Pavilion. The investigators left with 'the strong impression we had been imposed upon'.

The Pavilion in 1870.

Footsteps in the tunnels

The Sussex-based ghost hunter Andrew Green succeeded in obtaining more details about phenomena in the tunnels between the Pavilion and the Dome later in the 1970s. Although no-one had reported seeing an apparition, there were accounts of unexplained noises. An official at the Pavilion assured both Andrew Green and Frank Hennig of BBC Radio Brighton that several maintenance engineers had reported the sound of regular footsteps being heard in the passage leading to the Dome. One of the men was so convinced that he had been joined by an unknown 'helper' that he called out, 'What do you want?' only to find the tunnel empty, yet the footsteps continued for a short time until fading away. It is possible that the feelings of a presence and the perception of strange noises may be explained by the misinterpretation of natural sounds or auto-suggestion in a spooky environment. However, the reports became so numerous that several investigations were conducted, though no further light was shed on the mystery. On two other occasions the apparition of a woman in a shawl was allegedly seen in the tunnel and another story told of a figure of a soldier being glimpsed.

The White Lady

More evidence of a haunting by the White Lady was also obtained by local author John Rackham and detailed in his book *Brighton Ghosts and Hove Hauntings* (2001). His study revealed a pattern over the years of individual staff seeing a white lady in the building at night. As with so many white lady ghosts the details of her identity are a mystery, though theories have ranged

The Dome, haunt of the White Lady.

from Martha Gunn to Mrs Fitzherbert or some other mistress of George IV. The widespread nature of such apparitions – both in Brighton and many other parts of the UK – has led some researchers to question whether such apparitions are in fact actually connected with any human individual who may have lived or died at the place where they are seen to appear.

An alternative hypothesis has been advanced in recent years that spectral white lady apparitions may be a form of archetypal hallucination, representing the *genus loci* or 'spirit of a place'. Rather than arising from a particular deceased individual, such apparitions seem to be closer to an idea or symbol. Apparitions such as white ladies seem to be associated with particular landscapes, which trigger responses at a deep level of consciousness, in the form of visions or waking dreams. Such apparitions may be connected with the more exotic female apparitions of folklore and religion such as banshees, goddesses or angels. As such, they may be a construction of the unconscious mind stimulated by psychic forces that operate both internally and externally on the brain of the witness. It is postulated that these apparitions are subjective, in that they exist within the mind of the observer, but they also appear to have a degree of objective existence in that they recur at the same place to a succession of different witnesses, sometimes many years apart. The psychologist Carl Gustav Jung considered that: 'It not infrequently happens that the archetype appears in the form of a spirit in dreams or fantasy-products, or even comports itself like a ghost.' Could the White Lady of the Dome be an example of such landscape-induced imagery, conjured up amid the fantastic architecture of site?

Sir Charles Hockaday Dick

Among other ghosts connected with the Pavilion is the spectre of Sir Charles Hockaday Dick, one-time keeper of the Brighton Museum. The shade of Sir Charles is said to walk disconsolately in the grounds. He died in 1876 having become a vexatious litigant in the last few years of his life, obsessed with a debt owed to his family which stretched back centuries. His branch of the Dick family were once important and wealthy nobles close to King Charles I. His ancestor Sir William Dick had lent some £50,000 to the monarch. The money was never repaid by the Crown and over the centuries the fortunes of the Dick family dwindled to the extent their names disappeared from the directories of aristocrats and nobles compiled in later, class-obsessed centuries. Convinced that there was a fortune to be reclaimed, Sir Charles began letters and law suits against successive Governments demanding the return of the money. However, his claims were dismissed and no remedy was forthcoming from the courts after such a long period. Despondent at his lack of success he sank into alcoholism and lost his post at Brighton Museum. Thereafter he was found frequenting taverns 'overwhelmed by a melancholy that liquor alone could blot out'. What remaining money he had was drunk away and when he died in 1876 he was reputedly found with no more than a sixpence (two and a half pence in modern currency) in his wallet. To avoid a pauper's funeral his funeral expenses were covered by a Brighton townsman, Sir John C. Burrows.

Other traditions also have the ghost of Sir Charles appearing at Port Hall, a house with battlemented balustrades near the site of the old Brighton Grammar school; yet another site for his perambulations is Dyke Road just outside Post Hall Cottage, the oldest house on Dyke Road, on his way to the Pavilion.

The Theatre Royal

Across the road from the Pavilion and Dome stands Brighton's second-most famous theatre, the Theatre Royal. Like many theatres around the country it has a reputation for being haunted and stories of ghostly experiences have featured in the press for a number of years. Whether there is a connection between the Grey Lady of the Theatre and the White Lady of the Dome is unknown, but witnesses included two former managers, Mr Melville Gillam who saw her at the Royal in 1960 and Mr Jack Keates who saw her in a dressing room ten years later. Some writers have sought to positively link the Grey Lady with the ghost of Sarah Bernhardt who made a number of appearances at the theatre in 1894, though as researcher Andrew Green put it, 'why this great French actress should choose to haunt this theatre is a mystery'.

The Grey Lady was reputedly seen by an usherette in 1981 and in August 1982 she was seen by Anne Flood who was acting as wardrobe mistress. Whilst engaged in the laundry room she saw a figure of a woman about five foot six inches tall and aged between fifty and sixty. Over the woman's head was some grey veiling. Mrs Flood told the press, 'I had the immediate feeling it was a dead person. She had silvery hair and a commanding presence. She was visible for about a minute.'

An appearance of the Grey Lady is considered to be an omen of good fortune and this was certainly the reaction to a sighting which occurred on Sunday 21 October 1984, prompting the headline 'Royal's Lucky Ghost Spotted' in the *Brighton and Hove Gazette and Herald* two days later. One of the actresses, Mrs Sylvia Randall, was backstage during a technical rehearsal about 5 p.m. when she saw an unknown woman in dressing room number one. Mrs Randall's initial thought was that she was an intruder. She noticed the figure was wearing a long white dress with puffed sleeves, had brown curly hair and looked about twenty-five years of age. She returned to the room seconds later only to discover the lady had vanished completely.

In February 2002 an apparition of what may have been the Grey Lady was seen by the young son of a couple attending a performance, who asked his parents who was 'the tall lady in funny

The Theatre Royal.

old clothes'. She appeared to be sitting on a prop box at the side of a stage and the boy's parents later admitted to seeing 'something in a vague shape in the corner.'

It seems that on one occasion the phenomena in the theatre may have spread to an adjoining property. In October 1979 the *Brighton and Hove Gazette and Herald* carried the amused headline Knock, Knock! Who's there?' and asked if a poltergeist was haunting Leadbelly's Hamburger restaurant next to the Theatre Royal. Manager Pat Sullivan reported the mysterious movement of objects including a knife which flew at but fortunately did not strike his eldest daughter Vanessa. According to Mr Sullivan the knife simply '...came from nowhere'. A set of till keys also mysteriously disappeared only to re-appear on a carpet which had previously been taken up in the search for them. These accounts are consistent with many other accounts of poltergeist-propelled objects. Disturbed objects are rarely seen to begin moving, usually being experienced either in flight or their movement inferred on inspection or discovery; even more remarkably objects can appear to materialise from out of thin air.

Another interesting aspect of the case was that staff at the Theatre Royal reported hearing strange knocking sounds coming from the restaurant between 4 and 5 p.m. during the same period. 'We don't know where they are coming from,' Mr Sullivan was reported as saying. However, whilst raps and knocks are common features of poltergeist disturbances, the regular timing of the phenomena might suggest a mundane explanation such as a periodic problem with water or heating pipes. Whatever the case, the cause was never discovered. The restaurant has since closed and been replaced by another eating establishment who have reported no further problems.

FOUR

HAUNTED HOTELS AND PUBS

The reputation of Brighton as a sea-side resort has ensured the presence of a large number of hotels, guest houses and inns for the accommodation of visitors and a correspondingly large number of public houses, taverns and clubs to provide alcoholic refreshment. Many of the hotels and numerous pubs have stories of hauntings and the following are a selection of some of the most intriguing historical and contemporary stories.

The Royal Albion Hotel

No less than three different and colourful candidates have been put forward for the identity of the ghost which haunted certain parts of the Royal Albion Hotel. Now owned by the Britannia Hotel Chain this imposing building which stands opposite Brighton Pier will forever be linked by mystery seekers with the strange death of one of the pioneering figures of the early days of psychical research and what has become popularly known as 'ghost hunting'. This was the talented investigator Edmund Gurney whose lifeless body was discovered in a bedroom on the afternoon of Saturday, 23 June 1888.

Certainly, one particular bedroom of the Royal Albion had a 'haunted' reputation well into the 1980s. The atmosphere proved so cold 'even on the most sweltering of summer days' that it was eventually divided into two separate rooms. Thereafter, the temperature became normal. Such experiences prompted speculation that the feelings might be due to the returning ghost of Edmund Gurney but regrettably for this theory confirmation is not possible since the hotel registers from before 1922 no longer exist. Thus, it is not known for certain if this could have been the room in which Gurney died.

A sensitive and enthusiastic man in life, Edmund Gurney had thrown himself into psychical research with a passion from the foundation of the Society for Psychical Research six years before his death, conducting experiments in telepathy and extensive research into apparitions. In London on the Thursday before his death Gurney had received at his home what has been termed a 'mysterious letter' asking him to go to Brighton. He travelled down to Brighton the next day and checked into the Royal Albion Hotel for the Friday night. On the afternoon of the Saturday his door was found to still be locked. On receiving no answer to repeated knocks and calls the hotel staff forced entry. Gurney was found lying dead in bed with a pad of chloroform across his face. There was no note and an absence of any identification by which his body could immediately be identified.

The mysterious circumstances of Gurney's death were the subject of a controversial book, *The Strange Case of Edmund Gurney* (1964) by the late Trevor Hall. Gathering rumours that dated back to the 1880s that Gurney had committed suicide, it offered the theory that Gurney – who was known to have depressive tendencies – had taken his own life on learning that two men whom he had positively tested for telepathy had in fact been cheating. The pair concerned were G.A. Smith of Brighton and a journalist, Douglas Blackman, who confessed in 1908 and 1911 to cheating in the tests by means of a code. (It should be noted that G.A. Smith strongly disputed these accusations.) Trevor Hall proposed Gurney discovered the deceit whilst in Brighton and that the scandal was compounded by leading members of the Society for Psychical Research conspiring to conceal the fact at the inquest. Against this theory, it must be said that there is evidence to suggest that Gurney had suffered an accidental self-administered overdose of the drug which he had used to control neuralgic attacks. The verdict of coroner's jury was that Gurney had 'accidentally suffocated by an overdose of chloroform taken probably for the relief of pain.'

Furthermore, Gurney was then involved with investigating the haunted house in Prestonville Road, Brighton which is discussed in Chapter Two and there is little to suggest that he was pursuing the matter of the telepathy testing at the time. As for the mysterious letter, it may have been no more than the confirmation of his booking at the Royal Albion Hotel.

Predictably in the spiritualist atmosphere of the times, there were also rumours that communications were made by Gurney from beyond the grave. These were received from an American medium Mrs Piper and supposedly hinted at suicide, but even these only emerged as dubious second-hand stories. At this distance it is unlikely that the final truth will ever emerge.

Two other candidates have been put forward for the identity of the ghost at the Royal Albion. One is Harry Preston (1860-1936) who was responsible for refurbishing and preserving the Royal Albion Hotel in the early twentieth century. Later knighted, he gave his occupation as 'Hotel Proprietor' in *Who's Who* and was a well-known local character for many years. An even more extraordinary suggestion is that the ghost might be a self-styled occultist and magician Roslyn D'Onston who was also in Brighton at the time at the same time as Gurney, though D'Onston was more closely associated with the Cricketers inn in the Lanes.

D'Onston was later one of the more controversial suspects for the infamous Jack the Ripper murders which occurred in the autumn of the same year as Gurney died. The proponent of D'Onston as the Ripper was the late Melvyn Harris, a writer on crime and true mysteries and another outspoken sceptic regarding all things paranormal. Harris detested the occult and its self-proclaimed practitioners so it is perhaps not surprising that he put forward D'Onston as his candidate for the Ripper; there was also some contemporary speculation at the time that this might be the case. However, other scholars have cited numerous objections against D'Onston being the infamous Whitechapel killer. Nonetheless, in honour of the D'Onston theory, the Royal Albion Hotel was selected as the scene of the Jack the Ripper convention for scholars and students of the crimes in October 2005.

Other phenomena reported at the Royal Albion in the 1980s were doors opening and closing by themselves, sudden temperature drops and cold breezes. Interference with electrical equipment

The Royal Albion Hotel.

Sir Harry Preston and staff at the Royal Albion.

Roslyn D'Onston, occultist and Jack the Ripper suspect.

of differing kinds is a feature of many alleged haunted houses and such problems were reported at the Royal Albion. On occasions the hotel lift moved up and down by itself, with a Sunday evening being the most common time for this and other unusual incidents. Anomalous electrical fields might also generate strange static sensations and feelings of 'goose bumps' and one wonders if these may have contributed to the fire which damaged the hotel in November 1998. It is an old superstition in some parts of the world that haunted houses eventually suffer fires and burn down (this would make a fascinating study for an actuarial-minded researcher!) which has led some researchers to speculate if there is an energy involved in haunting phenomena which moves along the electromagnetic spectrum and eventually ends in the infra-red, generating heat with resultant outbreaks of fire. If so, this might explain why manifestations in the last twenty years have been low-key and may have ceased entirely following the 1998 fire. Although the current management are aware of 'stories of Sir Harry Preston's ghost being seen years ago' their official position at March 2006 is that the manifestations have ended.

A suicide's ghost at the York Road lodging house

One of the best authenticated hauntings at a local guest house took place some ten years after Gurney's mysterious death. It has long been believed that a sudden death, particularly the self-violence of suicide, can leave a lasting legacy and the haunting at the lodging house in York Road, Hove in 1898 is a classic example.

York Road, Hove, c. 1898.

On 22 March 1898 a lady named Mrs Mary O'Donnell took lodgings with her daughter at the guesthouse. Mrs O'Donnell intended to stay for a lengthy period and initially congratulated herself on their choice of lodging. But on the very first evening in the house she felt what she described as 'a strange sense of cold and gloom' pervading the atmosphere in her bedroom and 'an unaccountable feeling of desolation.' Her first thoughts were that she had perhaps caught a cold and so she requested that a fire be made up in her room by the maid. She retired to bed but had only been lying down a short time when she began to hear noises from upstairs. It sounded as though someone was walking around upstairs and the noises continued throughout the night.

When the maid came in at 8 a.m. Mrs O'Donnell asked her about the sounds, only to be told, 'No-one is upstairs, all the house is vacant.' This was confirmed by the landlady but Mrs O'Donnell remained certain that she had heard the noises and although she had never believed such things she found herself thinking that the lodging house was haunted. That night the noises came again, even louder. It proved impossible to sleep and the next day Mrs O'Donnell felt ill. On the third night of her stay Mrs O'Donnell had a large fire made up and kept a night light burning. She retired about 11 p.m. with her daughter wishing her goodnight.

With a thrill of terror Mrs O'Donnell heard the same footsteps again from upstairs. As she lay in bed she watched the fire for a long time until a feeling arose that she should look towards the wall. Giving into the impulse, she turned to see a horrifying scarecrow-like figure standing by her bedside. It appeared to be of a slight, dark man with very small hands, dressed in a tattered black suit. One arm of the figure pointed towards the adjoining room, the other pointing at her, its hand close to her face. The phantom had its face averted but she noticed its head and arms were very dark.

Terrified by the apparition, Mrs O'Donnell gasped for breath and covered her face with the bedclothes to shut out the horrible vision. After a while, she ventured to look again, thinking it was all imagination. Her detailed account vividly conveys the alarm she felt at the spectre: 'There it still was. I shrieked for terror and called out 'Oh my God, what is it?' and put out my left hand as if to feel if it was real, but imagine my horror as I was gripped by the icy hand of death.'

Mrs O' Donnell fainted and remembered no more until her daughter came into her room at an early hour. Mrs O'Donnell was unable to speak for a long time but eventually told her dreadful story. Her daughter immediately offered to change rooms, insisting all the time that her mother should not sleep in the room again.

Accordingly, the next night Mrs O'Donnell settled into the room previously occupied by her daughter. She locked the door but found she could not sleep. During the middle of the night Mrs O'Donnell was startled to see the figure of what she described as a '…small dark, gentlemanly young man' walk into the room. The figure announced, 'Oh, so you have the Scotchman's room', smiled at her and then turned and walked out without a further word or gesture. For her part, Mrs O'Donnell found the incident, 'all so strange and dreadful' but did not suffer the terror of the night before.

However, she was determined to discover what lay behind the visits of the spectre and asked friends in Brighton if they knew anything about the house. Her friends were greatly startled, immediately asking, 'Can this be the suicide house?'. Mrs O'Donnell tackled the landlady who initially denied everything. However, she eventually admitted the truth about the incident after Mrs O'Donnell heard similar stories from local traders. The suicide had been by a young man who was the member of a family which had lodged at the house for a period and had slept in the bedroom first occupied by Mrs O'Donnell. She learned that the young man had been ill and one morning had suddenly thrown himself out of the window of the room. His clothes were torn into shreds as he fell. On talking with the landlady, and her son who waited at table, the description of the figures she had seen corresponded with the physical appearance of the young man who had died. She also learned that the landlady was reluctant to go upstairs by herself after dark. On enquiring about the meaning of the phrase 'the Scotchman's room', she learned that it had formerly been occupied by a young Scottish man who had since gone into service. He had been a great friend of the young man who had died.

What Mrs O'Donnell did not immediately discover was just how recently the suicide had occurred. Further inquiries proved that the ghost could be traced to a tragic death a mere six weeks before. The *Sussex Daily News* for 8 February 1898 recorded the details of the death of Walter Overton Luckman, formerly a clerk in the town of Brighton as reported at an inquest. Walter Luckman had been depressed and suffered from bad bronchitis and asthma all his life. Stricken by a very severe attack one Friday, he was confined to bed, and had been nursed by his mother. On the Saturday morning she had left him for a moment to go to her own room whereupon he suddenly got up and locked the door. She called his brother Arthur who forced the door open to see his brother in the process of climbing out on the window sill. Arthur had rushed to stop him but before he could reach him Walter had jumped out.

Rushing downstairs to the street, Arthur found his brother still breathing and helped carry him indoors but it was too late. Walter Luckman died very quickly afterwards. Medical opinion given at the inquest detailed that the deceased had fallen on his left side, breaking his arm. His head was quite uninjured save for a blow to the nose. The cause of death was certified as shock caused by the fall. Walter Luckman had no history of attempting suicide and had never threatened previously to do away with himself. The inquest jury had recorded a verdict of 'Suicide while of unsound mind'.

Mrs O'Donnell sent details of her experience to the Society for Psychical Research who checked the details in the case, including contacting her daughter and publishing the details in its *Proceedings* for December 1898. The story fits the classic pattern of many ghost stories, in which

SAD SUICIDE AT HOVE.

Mr. G. E. Hillman, Coroner for East Sussex, held an inquest yesterday at No. 58, York-road, Hove, touching the death of Walter Overton Luckman.

Arthur Overton Luckman, living at 58, York-road, Hove, said deceased was his brother, and was 24 years of age. He was formerly a clerk in the employ of Messrs. Robins and Sons, of Waterloo-street. He had suffered from asthma all his life, but on Friday week he had a very severe attack, which confined him to bed. He had also been a little delirious. His mother had been sleeping in the same room. On Saturday morning she left the room to go to her own apartment, and directly she reached her room she heard his brother lock the door. She called witness, who at once forced the door open, and saw his brother climbing on to the window-sill. He disappeared just before witness reached him. He was only dressed in his nightshirt at the time. Witness went downstairs, and, with the help of the servant, carried deceased indoors. He had never attempted to take his life before, and had not threatened to do so. When picked up he was breathing slightly, but died almost immediately after.

Mr. Richard Hughes, L.R.C.P., practising at Sillwood-road, Brighton, deposed to having known deceased for about fifteen years. Deceased had been subject to attacks of asthma, from which he used to suffer very severely. Witness had not seen him for two years or more. The brother came for witness on Saturday morning last, and told him what had happened. On going to the house he found the young man was dead. The cause of death he attributed to shock. Deceased had evidently fallen on his left side, as the left arm was broken, the head being quite uninjured, save for a blow on the nose, which might have been caused by striking against something in the fall. Witness was sure that the act was committed in a sudden attack of delirium.

The jury returned a verdict of " Suicide while of unsound mind."

Sussex Daily News' report of the suicide.

the newcomer or guest in an unfamiliar room has an eerie experience that is later considered to correspond with certain details of a tragedy which took place in the room at an earlier date. An interesting aspect of Mrs O'Donnell's story is that it would appear that she saw the ghost of the same person but in two different guises. Another unusual detail is that figure seemed to speak (in stories collected in the last two hundred years it is rare for an apparition to speak, though other sounds such as footsteps are quite common in reports from haunted houses).

If Mrs O'Donnell's experiences are taken as paranormal in nature, various hypotheses can be advanced. The traditional explanation of a ghost as a restless spirit might explain the manifestations including the materialisation of the spirit in different guises, in an attempt to communicate. An alternative possibility is that Mrs O'Donnell was receptive to psychic impressions which entered her mind on successive nights in the room when she was in a relaxed state. Having picked up energies or emotions left at the scene of the by some clairvoyant or telepathic process, her subconscious mind went on to create the dramatic apparitions and sounds which she experienced.

A ghost of the living at the Princes Hotel

It is commonly thought that ghosts represent the shades of deceased persons. However, for over a century it has been realised that many apparitions are those of living people. Just one such curious case of an apparition of a living person occurred near the former Princes Hotel in Brighton in 1922 and was seen by Lady Troubridge, the long-time partner of controversial writer Radclyffe Hall (1880-1943), whose novel *The Well of Loneliness* was the subject of an obscenity prosecution in 1928. Throughout much of their lives both women were deeply interested in spiritualism and psychic phenomena; in the early 1920s Radclyffe Hall served on the Council of the Society for Psychical Research for a number of years. Although present, Radclyffe Hall did not see the figure but she was able to confirm the course of events.

In August 1922 the pair were in Brighton for a short holiday. By their own admission their thoughts were far from psychical research at the time, Radclyffe Hall recording '…we were not thinking of psychical research, from which we were purposely enjoying a complete rest….we were in a relaxed holiday mood.' On 23 August Lady Troubridge and Radclyffe Hall stepped out of the Princes Hotel at 10.45 a.m. intent on meeting a friend (whom they gave the pseudonym Miss X). The purpose of the meeting was to get the advice of Miss X on a car which Radclyffe Hall was contemplating buying from a nearby garage.

Walking from the hotel along a set of mews towards the garage Lady Troubridge suddenly saw Miss X standing by the garage. She noticed that Miss X was unusually dressed wearing a thin dark navy blue suit and a man's black hat. In an account written later that day, she stated, 'She seemed to be standing either against the open glass door of the garage, or, it crossed my mind – without at the moment striking me as illogical, that I might be seeing her reflected in glass, as her figure appeared as I might say dark against a background of glass – and yet…..I not only saw her with normal distinctiveness, but in a way too detailed in my opinion to be possible for normal vision at some thirty feet away – and I am *very* short sighted … although it did not strike me at the time, when I described what I had seen to Miss Radclyffe Hall.'

Lady Troubridge exclaimed 'There's X' but her comment was met by bafflement by Radclyffe Hall. Lady Troubridge said that she saw X in the shop but looking again the figure had vanished. Lady Troubridge assumed that their friend had gone inside and on arriving at the garage asked after her, only to be told that she had not yet arrived. At this point Lady Troubridge realised that she had experienced an apparition. Having walked around the show room and satisfied herself that Miss X was not there, she remarked in a quiet voice in French to Radclyffe Hall, 'All the same, I saw her.'

Both women began to fear that the vision might be linked to some harm suffered by Miss X. Telling a motor engineer that they would return later both women set off in the direction of Miss X's home, agreeing to make a note of how she was dressed when they found her. Both women thought it improbable that she would be wearing the thin blue suit as Miss X said she had felt cold in it. For their part, the two women expected Miss X to be clad in tweeds as there was a biting wind that morning. On calling at Miss X's house they found her dressed in an identical fashion in the same suit and hat that Lady Troubridge had seen in her vision. Miss X stated that she had been worried that she would be late for their meeting and had put on the suit as it had been lying ready, together with the black hat. She stated that she had never worn the hat with that suit before.

On returning to the Princes Hotel later that day both Lady Troubridge and Radclyffe Hall wrote up the events of day, Radclyffe Hall recording that, 'I personally was absolutely convinced that she had seen Miss X or some part of Miss X, or some vision of Miss X as we approached that garage because the whole thing seemed so spontaneous and so natural'. These accounts were subsequently published in the *Journal* of the Society for Psychical Research in April 1921, as a case of a 'veridical apparition' being one which communicated verifiable information unknown to Lady Troubridge at the time.

The Census of Hallucinations conducted by the Society for Psychical Research in 1894 involved 17,000 questionnaires and received 2,272 affirmative replies. Of those experiencing visual apparitions, some 32 per cent reported seeing the form of a living person, exceeding the 14 per cent of those identified as being of dead persons with 33 per cent remaining unidentified. As a result much thought was given to ghosts arising as a form of telepathy between the living as much as anything to do with the dead; many such apparitions were reported as occurring at moments of trauma or the actual death of the individual concerned. Such cases became known as 'crisis apparitions'.

However, this did not appear to be the case with the phantom of Miss X seen by Lady Troubridge. For her part Miss X confirmed the matters in a written statement so far as they were within her knowledge. Beyond the fact that she had felt flurried and annoyed at being late for her appointment she had not been in any extreme state of illness, sleep or acute agitation at the time she was being seen elsewhere.

The Regency Hotel

This private hotel has enjoyed a reputation for being haunted for over twenty years, having been included in a haunted hotel guide in 1984 as a recommended place for a spooky break. Some confusion seems to have arisen with the identity of the ghost at the Regency Hotel having been inadvertently mixed up with the phantom of a crippled girl at the Regency Tavern (see below). The current owners do not speak of manifestations but photographer Anna Pearce stayed at the hotel in the

The Regency Hotel.

course of taking some of the photographs for this book. During the early evening of Saturday 27 January 2006 she experienced a strong sensation of a presence, and during the night awoke to the sensation of being shaken in her bed.

The Battle of Waterloo

Ghost stories seem to encourage myth-making and the process seems to have been at work with the story associated with the Battle of Waterloo pub in Rock Place. Around the year 1800 a highwayman is said to have ambushed the coach of the Mayor of Brighton and kidnapped his daughter who was travelling in the vehicle. The coachman gallantly tried to protect the young woman but was mercilessly shot down for his act of bravery. The highwayman made off with the girl who, it was claimed, was never seen again. Meanwhile, the coachman staggered mortally wounded into the inn (later to become the Battle of Waterloo) to raise the alarm, told his story and expired. In other versions both the Mayor and the coachman were shot dead.

Sensational stories involving the forcible abduction and ransoming of attractive young women certainly flourished in the eighteenth and early nineteenth centuries. Many involved highwaymen or gangs of organised criminals who could prove a very real danger to travellers on lonely, unpoliced roads. In yet other cases, the alleged kidnapping story provided a cover for an elopement or an embarrassing indiscretion with a man. Though women were usually the potential targets of abduction, in other tales the alleged kidnapping often formed part of elaborate plots to trap naïve, wealthy men for blackmail purposes. Such scenarios seemed a particularly potent threat to the male imagination at the time when the crimes of rape and abduction were capital offences and an accused person could not give evidence on his own behalf. Although proof of such conspiracies was scant this did not stop many in the legal establishment from treating such rumours with a depressing degree of solemnity and seriousness. As a result the female victims of genuine crimes were often treated with excessive suspicion when testifying in court and their evidence was frequently dismissed as untrustworthy.

The story told about the Battle of Waterloo pub and the kidnapped Mayor's daughter is almost certainly a legend from this time. Although the story has been told for decades no contemporary corroboration has surfaced to suggest that any such incident ever took place. It may be that the story was developed to 'explain' the appearances of a figure dubbed 'the coachman' who was seen by customers walking across the bar in the 1970s. The then licensees Tom and Peggy Butler never saw the apparition and claimed that it only appeared to customers. However, Tom Butler was prepared to say he had felt a presence in the pub from time to time. In 1996 a decorator reported seeing the figure of a tall man in a cloak 'walk or rather glide through the front door' whilst other stories from the mid-1990s onwards suggest that the phantom coachman had been joined by a ghostly woman in the pub.

The Blue Gardenia Club

The now closed Blue Gardenia Club in Queen's Square was a popular Brighton drinking spot and night club during the early 1960s. However, it was hit by crime and tragedy when Harvey Holford shot dead his twenty-one year old wife Christine, a former model, on 15 September

1962. Having fired six bullets into his wife from a revolver, Holford then unsuccessfully attempted suicide with an overdose of pills. In March 1963 at the Sussex Assizes in Lewes Harvey Holford was found guilty of manslaughter and sentenced to three years imprisonment

Many thought his conviction was the conclusion of the tragedy but within a few weeks the ghost of Mrs Holford was believed to be coming back to the kitchen of the Blue Gardenia Club in which she was shot. Among reported phenomena were lights which turned on and off by themselves and a cooker which was repeatedly found switched off of its own accord. Fish knives and forks were also found to have been moved and the pet poodle named Coco which belonged to the new owner Mrs Freida Nicholson showed reactions of fear near the kitchen and howled by the door every night. Coco became so distressed that Mrs Nicholson had to take her dog to stay with friends as her own sleep had become so disturbed.

The story reached the national press, with the *Sunday Mirror* publishing an account on 21 April 1963. Mrs Nicholson was quoted as saying: 'I don't believe in ghosts and spirits. I thought my staff had been interfering with things in the kitchen but they all deny touching anything.' As a result a spiritualist medium was called in to attempt to quell the manifestations. The medium turned out to be a rather robust character named Mr Cullen, a former sergeant major who convened a séance at the end of April 1963. He was quoted as saying, 'The spirits of people who die suddenly and violently are often earthbound. They carry on doing the same things they always did and this is why I am sure this is Christine's spirit. For instance, I understand that fish was one of her favourite foods.' He insisted that the séance would be to make contact with the late Mrs Holford and that it was not a form of exorcism.

The Blue Gardenia Club is now long closed; and no further reports have been made, so it seems that the visit by the medium restored a sense of calm to the premises that have occupied the site ever since.

The Lion, St James Street

Nearly thirty years before the killing of Christine Holford at the Blue Gardenia a similar crime occurred at The Lion public house in St James Street when Harry Metcalfe, landlord of The Lion, shot dead his wife with three bullets from a revolver. Unlike the Holford case Metcalfe saved sufficient ammunition to commit suicide. Turning the gun on himself he ended his life rather than face a capital trial for murder.

After the double tragedy The Lion acquired a reputation for being haunted with local people speaking of the ghosts of the couple haunting the pub for many years afterwards. At one time it was thought that alterations to the property may have put paid to the haunting but many residents and customers have been convinced of a haunting presence at the pub. Local writer John Rackham obtained two interviews with former licensees about phenomena in the pub for his book *Brighton Ghosts, Hove Hauntings* (2001). During the 1980s and 1990s doors opened and closed by themselves; strange sounds and drops in temperature were reported by successive licensees. Another experience involved the sighting of a grey shape seen in an upstairs lounge by a lady resting on a settee. Such an account reflects the tendency of apparitions to appear when the mind is in a relaxed state and almost never when the person is thinking about ghosts at the moment the experience occurs.

The Regency Tavern

Not far from the Regency Hotel is the Regency Tavern. The building was originally a dairy and a cobbler's shop, originally established in 1893 and incorporated into the building in an extension in the 1930s. One ghost is said to be a crippled girl who died after jumping from an upstairs room in the late nineteenth century. She had supposedly been locked in her room as a punishment for some trivial wrong-doing. Mistakenly believing she could smell gas and fearing either poisoning or an explosion, the girl leapt in a panic from the window to the street below with fatal results.

The second ghost in the Tavern is described as 'a tall and slender grey-haired lady' who held the pub for many years. Eventually after her death, the pub was run by her sons who went on to open a successful chain of pubs along the south coast. Her ghost is seen on the first floor. Although the landlady was reputedly a pleasant and sociable lady in life, her presence after death was considered so terrifying to cats and dogs that none which entered the Regency 'could ever be persuaded to visit the first floor without bristling collar or arched back.' A visit by a medium is said to have laid the ghost but as in so many cases the effects proved only temporary or it may be that the presence switched its attentions to the cellar. During the 1980s dogs were reportedly reluctant to enter the cellar.

The current licensee Nicola Fairest who took over in 2005 has not had firm ghostly experiences in the pub despite a desire to do so. She lives in hope with the nearest to date being fleeting glimpses of a dark shadow from the corner of her eye on occasions when down in the cellar, '...but I couldn't be 100% certain what it was,' she stated in March 2006. However, in contrast to the earlier experiences with pets in the cellar her own dog seems happy to enter and certainly registered no adverse reactions in an experiment to test the atmosphere conducted on 28 March 2006.

Local stories aver that the pub also has a modern ghost, that of Mrs Jackie Penfold, the landlady at the Regency Tavern. Mrs Penfold died of a heart attack in 1990 during an outbreak of football violence when hooligans smashed windows along the side of the pub; a real example of the phenomenon of being 'scared to death'. It can be difficult to convict for murder or manslaughter in such cases and it is possible the tragedy might have boosted whatever residual psychic energy lingers in the building.

Albert at the Prestonville Arms

One of the most consistent features of pub ghosts both in Brighton and all round Great Britain are mild poltergeist tricks and pranks. These typically include moving or breaking glasses or ashtrays, tampering with beer taps and barrels, touching bar staff and making curious sounds. Often these phenomena appear to be examples of psychokinesis involving a mysterious energy generated from the subconscious minds of pub staff arising from stresses of the licensed trade. Nonetheless, this may not be the complete explanation of all cases because of the persistent nature of certain manifestations, which seem to continue regardless of changes in staff. There is rarely any precise information as to the likely identity of the haunting presence which, together with the playful nature of many of the manifestations, often lead to it being given a friendly nick-name.

Prestonville Arms in Hamilton Road is said to have an invisible ghost dubbed 'Albert' who was blamed for moving bottles noiselessly around the cellar during the hours of darkness, so

The Regency Tavern.

that '…the results of its nocturnal labours are plain to see in the morning' according to the late Jack Hallam in his book *The Haunted Inns of England* (1972), the first national survey of haunted pubs. However, it seems that 'Albert' has not been active since the 1960s.

The Oak

No names are known for the haunting presences at the Oak nor have they yet been dubbed with any nick-names. However, manifestations have been occurring at the Oak since 2004 when the current licensees took over. Somewhat sceptical they are nonetheless aware of noises from the cellar which have no ready explanation; even more remarkable has been the shifting of heavy metal beer barrels. These mirror reports from a number of cellars of other Brighton pubs over the years. Interestingly, a pet Labrador shows a strong dislike to parts of the cellar.

The pub dates from the early nineteenth century and has previously been a guesthouse. The unexplained movement of a middle barrel in a set in the cellar was noticed in January 2006. The barrels are extremely heavy and thoughts of how this could have happened of its own accord, 'is enough to make the hairs on the back of the head stand on end' according to the licensees

Above: *The Oak.*

Left: *The cellar of The Oak.*

Like many other haunted properties there have been mild problems with the electrical fixtures including the triggering of an alarm system and minor poltergeist tricks. Manager Robert Spencer experienced a strange incident when serving up some cheese and biscuits. He put down the plate for a moment only to witness the cheese knife literally 'jump off the plate' without any discernible cause. The incident occurred in daylight and was also witnessed by several customers. Small objects have been disturbed and 20p pieces have mysteriously appeared

Local resident Lara Robins works at the Oak and often comes in between 4 and 5 a.m. to clean and prepare the pub for the day ahead. Lara considers that there could be at least two separate presences. She has often had the sensation of someone standing behind her watching when working upstairs; she has the impression that it is a man in his early fifties and is not at all troubled by the feeling. The upstairs part of the pub seems neutral or even friendly. In January 2006 she heard the sound of old-fashioned classical and pre-war dance music being played in the building, an incident which she found puzzling rather than alarming. In contrast, the cellar parts of the building exude a strong, sometimes malign presence which makes working there alone uncomfortable.

The Stagg Inn

By coincidence, another entity nick-named Albert (see Prestonville Arms) was active at the 300 year old Stag Inn in Upper Bedford Street. One theory is that the 'impish joker' of the Stagg Inn is the spirit of a former landlord who detests modern beer. The theories of a phantom landlord were encouraged by the description of the ghost given by Joe Protheroe, who saw it soon after his father-in-law Bill Harman took over the pub in 1979. He saw a figure of a tall man in an apron with a black band around each arm standing in the kitchen and came running upstairs in fright. Later the same figure was seen in the corridor by Mr Harman and over the next four years there were persistent problems with beer taps.

The landlord theory has been postulated as the 'reason' why the entity targets the more modern features of the pub. Real ale is never interfered with, '…only your modern gas filled frothless liquid inflames Albert's spectral wrath', according to ghost and pub enthusiast Roger Long in his book the *Haunted Inns of Sussex*. However, there seems to have been no attempt by later licensees to establish his identity or obtain any coherent message by way of séances or mediumistic communication. Although the current licensees who took over in November 2005 have been told many stories about the pub they do not intend to pursue the matter of Albert's identity further.

The area around Brighton also has many other allegedly haunted inns and hotels. Two of the most famous are the Rottingdean Club and Hangleton Manor.

Cary Grant's Ghost At The Rottingdean Club?

One of the most extraordinary claims for the identity of any hotel ghost in the Brighton area has been made for the apparition and haunting presence at the Rottingdean Club, a hotel near Brighton. Although parts of the building date back to 1530, inflated stories suggested that the ghost might be none other than the sophisticated movie star Cary Grant (1904-1987). The story made national news in January 1989 when journalists claimed that 'suave Cary … has become a regular sight in the bar, the cellars and in Room Nine – his old bedroom.' Grant had a great affection for the hotel on his trips to England and on one occasion tried unsuccessfully to buy it.

The identification of the ghost as Cary Grant seems to owe more to wishful thinking and exaggerated reports of a sighting of a man in a raincoat in the cellar, although a chef named Jeremy Goodchild was quoted as saying, 'I have seen him several times. He was grey-haired and wearing a raincoat.' The same apparition was witnessed by a member of the bar staff named Lucinda Saunders who was down in the cellar one day and saw a figure in a raincoat sorting through bottles. She initially believed it to be the figure of the then owner Don Goodchild but he was found to be elsewhere in the building at the time. He was reported to have said. 'I hadn't been near the cellar, and I didn't believe in ghosts – now I have to.'

Given the resemblance of the ghost to the owner Don Goodchild there remains scope for it to have been an apparition of the living. Certainly, a sceptical approach was taken by Tom Perrott, chairman of the Ghost Club who was asked to comment on the case based on years of investigations in haunted pubs. However, he did not rule out the possibility of a haunting. Doubts about the story have not prevented its repetition and it continues to appear in guides to Brighton and articles on local ghosts. However, the current owner Jo Pratt who took over in 2001 confirmed in March 2006 that nothing has occurred in recent years, 'but we live in hope'.

Hangleton Manor Inn

The ancient Hangleton Manor near Hove had a long-standing reputation for being haunted before its conversion into a hotel and restaurant in 1982. In November 1964 the partly derelict Manor was reported to be attracting enthusiastic boys from a local grammar school intent on a spot of ghost hunting. Stories in circulation claimed that the building was haunted by a 'Lady Jane' who was said to have thrown her unwanted baby from an upstairs window. The ghost of Lady Jane was said to have been seen climbing the stairs. Other tales told of disembodied white hands fluttering in or near the building. Other accounts told of a noise like a game of skittles being played in an upstairs corridor.

A remarkable manifestation reported during the 1970s was the appearance a piece of phantom clothing, 'the skirt of a brown silk dress' sweeping through part of the building. As well as being seen, the phantom dress was also heard rustling by other witnesses. Although bizarre, the experiences are reminiscent of other ghost sightings around the UK. In the last forty years there have been reports of phantom trousers being seen in a field in Dorset and the cellar of a pub in Newmarket, a pair of grey striped trousers gliding through a sitting room in a house in Surrey and pair of corduroys standing by themselves in a shop in Devon.

Claims are made that the dress was worn by a Saxon girl who came to the house and was seduced by the Lord of the Manor. Alas for tradition, history renders this impossible since the Manor House dates from around 1550, nearly 500 years after the disappearance of Saxon wenches, and silk was not introduced until the seventeenth century. A slightly more plausible candidate for the wearer of the phantom dress is Mrs Fitzherbert, the lover of the Prince Regent in the eighteenth century. Mrs Fitzherbert was reputed to have visited the Hangleton Manor in her lifetime but there is nothing beyond romantic fancy to attribute this otherwise anonymous gown to her presence.

Hangleton Manor, early twentieth century.

More remarkable stories were collected in the 1970s from former employees who stated a female phantom in the building caused weird rappings from behind wood panelling and that ghostly cries of 'a tortured soul' were heard at night. Demolition fears at the time even stoked local concern that the spectres might begin to haunt the village instead! Such noises might easily be attributable to either directly to owls or foxes or their attacks on other wildlife such as rabbits, but occasional stories of doors opening and closing by themselves continued into the 1990s.

FIVE

THE GHOSTS OF PRESTON MANOR AND PRESTON MANOR OLD CHURCH

Best experienced when the grounds are quiet or seen on a cold winter's day, the visitor to Preston Manor will not be surprised to learn that it has been generating accounts of ghostly manifestations for over a century. Set a little away from the centre of the city, Preston Manor is not an imposing building but it is the nearest thing to a stately residence – albeit one of modest proportions – which Brighton can claim. Although not a striking residence visually it has an air of private solitude, strengthened by the presence of the ancient Preston Manor old church in its grounds and an expanse of parkland. Even though the green swards have been transformed into a modern recreation ground it is possible to feel a sense of separation and an atmosphere of isolation, ideal to fostering psychic impressions in the sensitive mind.

History indicates that a house was built upon the site of Preston Manor as long ago as 1250 and parts of the old foundations were incorporated into the construction of 1738. From 1794 onwards Preston Manor was owned by the Stanford family who continued to occupy part of the building through to the twentieth century, along with the MacDonald family to whom they were related through marriage. In 1925 Sir Thomas Stanford executed a deed of gift to transfer Preston Manor to Brighton Corporation upon the death of himself and his wife. After both had died Preston Manor accordingly entered into public ownership in 1932 and it has been maintained by the Borough ever since.

Preston Manor today

The White Lady

Stories of a ghost known as the White Lady or 'the Woman in White' haunting both the Manor and the surrounding area have been in circulation for over a century. Manifestations of the White Lady seem to have been at a peak in the 1890s when sightings were so frequent that they reputedly averaged one a month and were very much taken for granted by local people. The Manor at the time was an important centre for local social life. Accounts of the haunting during this period were published in the early 1920s and further details were also gathered in 1934 in interviews undertaken by a member of the Society for Psychical Research, two years after the Manor was taken over by the Brighton Corporation.

Typical of the experiences was that of Miss Lily MacDonald who was living at the Manor in October 1896. One day Miss MacDonald was in the process of changing a new lampshade in the drawing room, when suddenly the figure of a woman in white with golden hair entered the room and walked towards her, as if to speak. With considerable presence of mind Miss MacDonald tried to grasp the apparition but her hand passed right through it and it vanished away. Another witness to the White Lady was her sister, Di MacDonald (later Mrs Magniac) who had come in feeling hot from a vigorous game of tennis and saw a woman standing on the staircase looking towards her. At first she thought it was one of the maids but then realised it was a stranger. She was about to ask who the woman was when the figure mysteriously disappeared in front of her.

On another occasion at the same period, a friend of the family suffered an unpleasant experience whilst staying in the north-west bedroom. Mrs Magniac recalled in 1934 that one night a Mrs Studd came into her bedroom in a state of terror saying she could not sleep in the room any more. Mrs Studd had awoken to see a hand and arm with no body attached moving up and down one of the columns of the four poster bed. She declined to sleep in the room any more and asked to remain with Mrs Magniac through the night even if she had to lie on the floor. Mrs Studd left the Manor the next day.

Perhaps the most extraordinary sighting came from a Colonel Stanford who stated that he had not only seen the White Lady but actually spoken with her. On witnessing the White Lady for himself he was so astonished that he decided to ask her who she was and what she wanted. According to Colonel Stanford the ghostly lady replied to his question stating, 'I was a Religious' and told him that she had been denied a Christian burial and could find no rest until her remains were discovered. Then the apparition vanished. The Colonel's story – unlikely as it sounded – fuelled speculation that the White Lady must be the spirit of a nun.

Apart from visual apparitions there were a number of accounts of strange noises at Preston Manor and also of peculiar poltergeist tricks. These consisted of the cutting of diamond patterns in clothing hung in a particular cupboard. Of course, this might have been attributable to a human prankster but it is an interesting detail that this and a number of other phenomena at the Manor all occurred in the Blue Room. As Harry Price noted in his classic work *Poltergeist Over England* (1945) many famous haunted properties have Blue Rooms which prove particularly conducive to manifestations. Examples included Borley Rectory, Essex; Ballechin House in Perthshire; Willington Mill on Tyneside and Calvados Castle. At Preston Manor it was noted that residents always found it impossible to keep the Blue Room locked.

The Séances

Once Colonel Stanford's story became known it was inevitable that the occupants of the Manor should try and communicate further with the entity. Spiritualism was very much in vogue at the time, so it is not surprising that attempts were made to summon the ghost at a séance, using the ouija board method on 11 November 1896.

Ada Goodrich Freer.

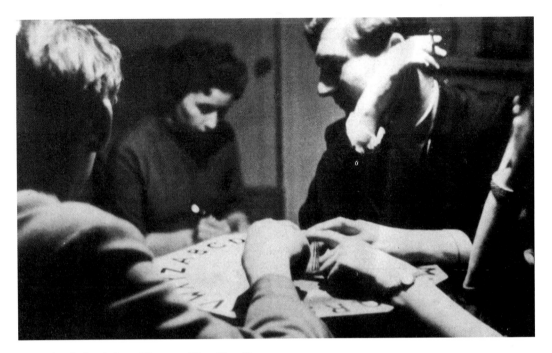

A ouija board séance (Courtesy of Tony Cornell).

That a séance certainly took place on this date in the Cleveland Room of Preston Manor is clear but precise details of the participants are somewhat confused. According to one account, both Mrs MacDonald and Miss Macdonald were both present together with a Mr Douglas Murray, 'Mrs Goodrich Freer' and a Miss X. Mrs Goodrich Freer, who was described in an account as 'a great spiritualistic medium now living in Dusseldorf' is an error. The lady undoubtedly referred to was an English woman Miss Ada Goodrich Freer who was active in psychical research but did not marry until 1905. Nor is it known that she claimed mediumistic gifts at this period but Ada Goodrich Freer did write voluminously in the 1890s on psychic topics as a regular contributor to the spiritualist magazine *Borderland* and also for the *Journal* of the Society for Psychical Research. This was under the pseudonym 'Miss X' which suggests that she and the mysterious Miss X at the Preston Manor séance were one and the same person. Ada Goodrich Freer was something of a sceptic towards mediums but accepted the reality of psychic happenings and even claimed clairvoyant powers herself.

The ouija board method involves the sitters resting their fingers upon a glass or a pointer on a board upon which the letters of the alphabet, numbers and the words 'yes' and 'no' are printed. The board was successfully patented in the United Sates in 1892 and many more people have manufactured their own in the years since. The word ouija comes from a combination of the French and German words for 'yes', *oui* and *ja*. The board is a variant of other boards such as the planchette which also uses a pointer or a pen used in other attempts at spiritualist communications. In most cases, the messages which come from the board are nonsense (G.K. Chesterton once wrote that the only thing that could be said for certain of the power behind planchette communications was that it told lies) and it seems that much – if not all – of the information comes from the subconscious mind. Often such experiments simply produce meaningless ramblings.

However, anecdotal stories suggest that use of ouija boards can trigger paranormal phenomena in the form of psychokinesis and their use should not be undertaken lightly or as some kind of game. Sensitive people have often been traumatised by their use and the messages which may emerge; in some cases people have needed medical treatment or believe their homes to have become haunted as a result. The séance in the Cleveland Room passed off without problems and indeed proved more successful than most. The board spelt out a number of messages and initially it seemed the spirits obviously objected to being disturbed for they told the sitters to go away. Nonetheless, the sitters persisted and when they asked to send the lady who haunted the mansion the reply came back that there were two. Encouraged by this message, the sitters asked their names and received the answer 'Agnes' and 'Caroline'. The communicator purported to be Caroline and claimed that she was a nun about 1535 with the surname of Marchmont and stated Preston Manor was occupied by a family named Marchant. When asked if she meant Marchmont or Marchant the answer came back that nuns had no names. When the sitters asked when Agnes died the board spelt out 'Curse her'!

Probing further, in response to questions the board claimed that Agnes had been excommunicated by the Church. When asked if she could be helped the message came through that it was too late this year but that Mass and prayers could be said on the first of November (All Saint's Day). It seems that this point 'Agnes' seemed to come through saying, 'Prove me innocent'. She stated she did no harm and was about the Manor all the time but did not know when anyone saw her and that her grave was outside. A man named Friar Martin was responsible for her excommunication. The messages also indicated there was a broken-down tunnel beneath the grounds and that the Manor had once been a monastery with 42 monks in its past.

Later in the séance a personality claiming to be 'Friar Martin' came through in messages spelt out by the board. The messages claimed that no crime was committed and that Agnes had done no wrong but he had caused her to be excommunicated. He also stated that she would find rest sooner than she thought. Interesting though the results of the séance had been, nothing was done afterwards as Mrs MacDonald did not think the messages justified taking up the stones of the Terrace on the off-chance that bones lay beneath it.

Discovery of the bones

However, events took an interesting turn when excavation work to repair drains at the Manor became necessary soon after. In what some took to be an apparent confirmation of the ouija board prediction, on the 29 January 1897 workmen digging a trench to restore the drains close to the south terrace of Preston Manor uncovered a skeleton. A Dr Blaber conducted an examination of the remains and considered they had belonged to a woman between forty-seven and fifty-five years of age and were over 200 years old. The bones were well preserved, although they had become stained orange in colour.

Their preservation was all the more remarkable because no trace of a coffin could be found. Disturbingly, the bones had not been laid out in an East-West alignment but merely piled in a hole. The discovery had all the hallmarks of a pit which had been dug for a corpse, which had been merely dropped in and quickly covered over rather than given a formal interment ceremony. It suggested the disposal of a murder victim or someone denied a Christian burial such as a suicide or an executed criminal.

Preston Manor old church.

Versions differ as to what happened next. According to one story, the bones were put into a box and interred in the churchyard and a plaque put up to commemorate their discovery; another story had the bones buried in secret by the gardener (or a gravedigger) who read the burial service over them. However, common to both stories is the accusation that the vicar of Preston Manor church, the Revd Riley, was extremely annoyed by the prospect of the bones being interred in his churchyard, perhaps suspecting they were from an unconsecrated burial. Apparently, the matter caused 'a feud between the Vicarage and the Manor House for some time after', or perhaps it was the issue of the séances which had incurred the displeasure of the vicar.

A further interesting development took place in May 1897 when Douglas Murray discovered from Sir William Richmond that a historical work entitled *Annals of Canterbury* recorded the founding of the Monastery of 'Priest Town' at the site by a member of the Tracy family. This seemed a further confirmation of the messages at the séance six months earlier. Murray believed that no-one at the séance could have known this information but it is possible it might have been inferred from frescoes in Preston Manor church. Painted frescoes existed inside, including one behind the pulpit depicting the martyrdom of Thomas Becket. The paintings were covered up on orders from King Henry VIII and forgotten about for 300 years until their rediscovery in 1830 during renovation. Unfortunately, the frescoes were badly damaged in a fire in 1906 which damaged the roof, organ and loft of the church though luckily some sketches of them survive. The possibility of a shrine or some kind of monastery at the site might therefore have been an inspired guess by someone at the séance.

One year later, on 29 January 1898, the anniversary of the discovery of the skeleton, a further séance was held. This was conducted by Douglas Murray and Miss Lily MacDonald in the Anne of Cleve's Room. Sister Agnes purported to come through and claimed that she was happy since her skeleton had been reburied in the churchyard. The message came through, 'I am content to rest happily, I can be her guide.' Asked whose guide she might be, the board replied 'Lily's'.

The discovery of the bones and their burial certainly seemed to have brought a cessation to the haunting. On 10 December 1898 Douglas Murray recorded: 'Mrs MacDonald tells me that since the reburial of Sister Agnes' remains in consecrated ground there have been no sort of phenomena at Preston Manor, no appearance of Sister Agnes (which occurred about every month or six weeks to someone in the house), no opening or closing of heavy mahogany doors by invisible agency, no noises as of rolling tubs under the drawing room, no cutting of diamond patterns in the new silk dresses when hung in a certain cupboard, nothing at all abnormal'. As a result Murray felt he could confidently declare, 'The ghost is laid and apparently at rest. This has been the case for nearly two years'.

In November 1903 a female figure in white with golden hair hanging down was seen by a lady known as Nurse Glasspool. She was employed to attend Mrs MacDonald who by this time had been suffering from an extended illness and was confined to bed. Between 2 and 3 a.m. the figure looked around the screen at the foot of Mrs MacDonald's bed and gazed intently at Nurse Glasspool and Mrs MacDonald. The next morning when she met Miss Lily MacDonald, the Nurse said 'Oh Miss, would you mind another time if you come in at night to see Mrs MacDonald, just speak to me. It rather frightened me you coming in and not saying a word.' In fact Miss MacDonald had not come in during the night, but she thought at once of the ghost of 'Sister Agnes' in her white dress. However, rather than alarm Nurse Glasspool further she simply assured her that on all future occasions she would inform her of any visit during the night.' Mrs MacDonald died at the end of the month and the apparition was interpreted as a sympathetic farewell visit to her from the ghost.

Later manifestations

The sighting by Nurse Glasspool was the last appearance of the White Lady according to the journal kept by Douglas Murray. Sightings of ghosts inside seem to have ended by the middle of the first decade of the twentieth century, although noises seem to have continued for a period. On one occasion during the spring, Mrs Magniac had gone upstairs about half past ten and went to bed in the Blue Room. About two in the morning she awoke with the strong feeling of fear and heard the clock strike the hour. She then heard a slight rustling sound which seemed to be coming towards the bed and the fender shook. Immediately afterwards she had the impression of something immensely evil leaning over her, giving deep sighs and groans. Mrs Magniac was too frightened to move or look. The experience seemed to go on for some minutes but may in reality have been a much shorter period. Then the sensation ceased and she heard the rustling again near the door, more shaking of the fender and then silence. (It is interesting to note the similarities between her experience and those reported at Prestonville Road in 1888 and at Down Terrace some seventy years later, mentioned in Chapter Two.)

In September 1930, a Mr R. Peregrine Birch of Twyford, Berkshire, recalled that years before he had stayed at Preston Manor and heard the 'most weird and uncanny noises generally in the middle of the night'. These seemed to issue from the big dress cupboard in the Blue Room. On one occasion he had also heard loud taps on the cupboard door and the shuffling of footsteps, causing him to hastily barricade the door. Like Mrs Studd he felt that he could not stay in the house again and a further experience sealed his resolve. He had retired to bed with a bad cold before dinner and a bright fire and four candles were burning in his room. He was reading a book just before 10 p.m. when the brass rings on the four-post bedstead began ringing against each other and the bed began to shake. He laid down his book and looked around and saw at the post opposite a man's dead arm and hand 'with cruel fingers clutching the post and moving outwards.' He let out a shriek and fled the room, refusing to stay in it thereafter.

However, by the 1930s the haunting of the Manor seemed to have ceased completely as though the energy behind the haunting had faded away. Lady Thomas Stanford even wrote to her son saying she knew nothing personally about the haunting of Preston Manor House and claimed that no-one had ever seen an apparition. Indeed, it seems that over the next four decades the Parkland and church of Preston Manor became the focus of psychic activity. It was not until 1975 that interest in the haunting of Preston Manor was briefly rekindled. In that year a visitor claimed that he had seen a ghost dog run through rooms and disappear. The description of the spectral dog appeared to fit that of Kylin, a pet dog owned by Lady Thomas Stanford shown in a picture in the hall. Nonetheless, there were suspicions on the part of staff that the sighting was a hoax.

Certainly, by the mid-1970s it seems that the once active haunting had dwindled to an uncomfortable feeling of a presence emanating from a corner cupboard in the back bedroom. In 1977 Marion Walker, the keeper of Preston Manor and Rottingdean Manor, stated that an unpleasant atmosphere was often felt in the room by visitors. In 1978 ghost hunter Andrew Green visited Preston Manor with a group of students from a parapsychology evening course. Many of them confirmed what one described as a 'mysterious sensation of unease' emanating from the corner cupboard. Rumours were in circulation that the manifestations related to 'scandalous behaviour' at the Manor before the death of Lady Stanford in 1932 but nothing ever came to light as to the nature of the allegations.

Hauntings in the churchyard

Stories of ghosts haunting the churchyard around Preston old church to the north-west corner of the Park have been in circulation since the mid-1950s. The church was originally dedicated to St Peter and St Paul and dates from around 1250. Between 1531 and 1878 it was classed as part of the parish of Hove under one priest.

It was reported in the *Brighton and Hove Gazette* at the end of September 1966, during the incumbency of the Revd Selwyn Gummer, that members of the choir had seen, 'a ghostly figure emerge from the south side of the church and disappear into the churchyard'. On another occasion, two people passing the church one Sunday evening saw a pair of women in medieval costume who passed by them and then turned and disappeared through a terracotta tombstone on the west side of the church. These sightings came some ten years after a ghost hunt organised as a light-hearted jape by a group of local boys. They took up position among the tombstones, hardly taking their vigil seriously. However, their laughter turned to terror when they saw a black hooded figure appear among the graves. They watched the cowled form cross the churchyard, only to vanish as inexplicably as it had appeared.

These spectres in the churchyard were considered to be quite distinct from the woman in white at the Manor House. Further sightings of apparitions of what has been taken to be a woman in a medieval dress occurred during the 1970s and again in the 1990s. It appears that on several occasions witnesses encountered a partly formed phantom which seemed to resemble a cream dress. These partially formed apparitions have been reported at other places, such as at Hangleton Manor Inn. There are also stories of a woman in white being seen on the nearby

Preston old church graveyard.

recreation ground late at night. To complete the collection of apparitions another story has the ghost of Sir Charles Stanford wandering near the southern corner of the churchyard where his ashes were buried.

In many ways, the haunting at Preston Manor fulfils the age-old stereotype of a house haunted by a spirit who has been denied proper funeral rights. Yet the historical details produced in the séances are dubious and unverifiable, whilst the disturbances in the Blue Room and the presence in the cupboard seem more like a description of a mindless energy, rather than a conscious entity. As so often with ghost phenomena an attempt to analyse experiences raises more questions than can be answered.

It may also be noted that Frank Usher in his article on Brightonin *50 Great Ghost Stories* (1971) gives an account of a haunted house which once faced Preston Park. Compared with the manifestations associated with the Manor and the parkland the phenomena were on a minor scale but the impact on the householder was a dramatic one. They occurred at a private residence called Whitchurch House where the mysterious opening and closing of French windows was repeatedly experienced. The remarkable aspect of the phenomena was that the doors were locked and bolted both before and after their movement. Although the housemaid had on two occasions attempted to stop the opening, the mysterious force was too strong and she was pushed back and forced to watch the windows open and close of their own accord.

The owner of the report dismissed the story as 'nonsensical rubbish' until persuaded to witness it for himself one morning at 6.30 a.m. Shaken by the evidence before his eyes his reaction was to immediately put the house on the market and move away from the area as soon as a purchaser was found.

SIX

A VARIETY OF HAUNTED PLACES AND SPACES

Ghosts are traditionally expected in royal residences, old manor houses, historic inns and private houses. But since the beginning of the twentieth century it has been recognised that a wide range of other and often mundane premises can become haunted, including shops, offices and factories, as well as modern roads and sites in the open air. Brighton and its environs proves to be no exception to this pattern.

The haunted furniture manufacturer

One of the best attested cases in Brighton was the haunting of the former premises of Bevan Funnell Ltd in Finsbury Road. A principal witness in the case was Mr Funnell, who was a town councillor at Hove and elected mayor in 1960. Adding to his credibility, he was also a special constable and the case ultimately merited an entry in a book *50 Great Ghost Stories* (1971) edited by John Channing and written by Frank Usher.

Phenomena began in the early hours, shortly after Bevan Funnell had acquired the property in 1952. Old pictures of the now demolished building show it had a gloomy look and this atmosphere seemed to be experienced within. Initially, the building was locked each night but local patrolling police would find doors unlocked, requiring the owner to return and lock them again. One night when the local CID had been called upon to investigate the repeated phenomena, all the officers accompanying the owner heard footsteps coming from a large room on an upper floor. The noises ceased immediately the door was opened. Perhaps little more might have been made of the incident, but for the fact that on the next few weeks identical incidents were reported. These increased in frequency to such a degree that members of the staff began to hear the sounds whilst at work and the phenomena took on a more interesting aspect.

One of the workmen saw a woman in black frock standing in the workshops. It was, as with many ghost sightings, so solid-looking in appearance that the workman thought it was a customer. He turned to Mr Funnell, to draw his attention to the fact that there was a customer

Brighton Aquarium and Palace Pier, early twentieth century.

who needed serving. When he glanced back the figure had vanished. On another day, a strong heavy perfume was smelt in a passage. This new phenomena continued for some days, often wafting through the building like invisible clouds. Mrs Funnell believed that it might be linked with earlier uses of building, including its role as a home for 'fallen women'.

Shortly after the perfume was first experienced, a heavy knitted cardigan was found in a cloakroom only to inexplicably vanish later. Although the smell and the appearance and disappearance of the garment could have had a normal explanation, the highlight of the haunting was an event which was wholly inexplicable unless caused by psychokinetic energy of a very unusual nature.

This was the self-operation of a typewriter which could be heard tapping when the office was empty. Someone suggested that a mouse might have been running over the keys, but the weight of such a creature could not have operated the keyboard. In 1953 a séance was held during which the mysterious sound of a number of people running about seemed to conclude the phenomena and, thereafter, all seemed quiet. By 1954 the haunting had been relegated to history and practically forgotten until the Sunday morning before Christmas when Mr Funnell received the shock of his life was he entered the office in which the typewriter had operated by itself. He saw a grey dark shape upon a desk. The shape was half-hooded and seemed only partly formed yet had a degree of density and substance. The impression Mr Funnell had was of a figure in the process of materialisation. The experience was accompanied by a feeling of malignancy and he fled the room, arriving home ashen-faced and shaking.

Ultimately, because of the sense of evil which accompanied the figure, an exorcism was conducted and this may have been what finally put paid to the phenomena. Bevan Funnell moved out of the building some years later and it was demolished and built over. However, according to notes compiled on the case in the 1970s by researcher Andrew Green, 'strange noises' were still being experienced in the flats occupying the site.

Old Brighton Evening Argus office, North Road

A busy newspaper office may not sound like the place for a ghost. As the journalist and ghost hunter the late James Wentworth Day once wrote, newspapermen and photographers are (or at least were) a sceptical bunch who believed in expense accounts and good living and likely as not to treat ghost stories with amusement or scorn. But according to a story collected by the late Andrew Green a 'really weird' phantom was seen by staff at the *Evening Argus* building in North Road. The building was a former laundry and gained a reputation in the early 1970s for being haunted by phantom footsteps. Stories also came from two photographers employed by the *Argus* at the time. One named Jerry Caswell, a sceptic when it came to the paranormal, claimed to have seen 'the figure of a one-armed highwayman' in an upstairs office whilst working late. The Chief Photographer Dennis Wixey, when working in the same office, also reported something unseen touching his back.

Shoe shop, Hilton Road

The former Hilton Shoe Shop on St James Street was haunted by a woman in a grey dress until the early 1980s. At least three members of staff and a customer reported seeing the apparition. 'She is just standing there at the top of the stairs', one young assistant stated, 'and as you look at her she just disappears.' Rather unusually for a ghost her appearances seemed limited to between 9 and 10 a.m. rather than later in the day or evening.

Like many apparitions, the identity of the phantom lady was a mystery. The only suggestion that was put forward was that she represented the shade of a former owner of a building which stood upon the site. As with the vast majority of apparitions, there was no cause for alarm and the figure was casually accepted as one of the features running with the property.

Brighton College

Apart from the Cambridge and Oxford colleges and some of the older boys' public schools, relatively few educational and learning establishments in Great Britain have any great traditions or reputations for being haunted. This is in contrast to the United States where a great many colleges and schools are said to have resident ghosts, perhaps linked to differences in story telling traditions and higher levels of violence.

As if to make up for this perceived deficit in Britain, Brighton College, founded in 1845 as a boy's school and now a mixed college, claims at least three spectres. These include a boy in a khaki uniform in the 1920s, thought to be a member of the Officer Training Corps once based at the school. He was perhaps one of the many former pupils of the school who fell in the First World War. Another ghost is said to be a former headmaster. He was headmaster of the school and has been reported in the grounds. Completing the trio is a Victorian Grey Lady seen inside the school; who she is or may have been remains a mystery.

Brighton College, The Avenue.

Brighton College, allegedly haunted by three spectres.

The Brunswick Arms restaurant (now closed)

The Brunswick Arms restaurant at 67 Ditchling Road was the scene of remarkable poltergeist incidents in 1974 when over two dozen saucers and other pieces of crockery were mysteriously lifted and then smashed during May and June of that year. Mike Wilde the owner of the building first experienced the so-called 'ghostly happenings' when 'a plate lifted itself out of a wall bracket, travelled four feet across the kitchen and smashed itself on the floor. Later a frying pan followed the same path.'

One explanation for the phenomena was put forward by Mr Charles Page of Sandgate Road, who lived on the premises over fifty years before. He felt that the ghost was that of his mother, whose violent second husband used to throw saucers and plates at her and the children. Mr Page felt that she was trying to make contact in an effort to establish where her last will lay hidden. Psychical researchers considered that poltergeist phenomena were more likely to emanate from the mind of a person under stress, particularly an adolescent or a person in middle age.

Equally, the fact that there might be something really inexplicable going on could not be discounted. Around a quarter of poltergeists seem to be persistent, place-centred rather than person-centred phenomena. These seem more akin to hauntings and continue irrespective of changes in residents. Certainly, the then Brunswick Arms saw a remarkable turnover in occupiers over the sixteen years to 1974. No-one stayed in the premises for more than 12 months during the entire period 1958 to 1974, perhaps suggestive of a pattern of earlier activity or of repeated unhappiness which might have generated poltergeist incidents.

A phantom vessel is said to be visible from Nicholas's Churchyard on 17 May

The churchyard of St Nicholas

Watch the churchyard on a night of the full moon and you may see a phantom horse galloping across the graveyard. Stand in the churchyard on the night of 17 May at midnight and you may see the spectral form of a medieval ship out to sea. So run two legends associated with Brighton's most prominent churchyard which surrounds the church of St Nicholas, the oldest building in Brighton, along Dyke Road.

Although often considered haunted locations it is a curious fact that churchyards and cemeteries rarely produce reliable sightings of apparitions. This absence of ghosts is perhaps even more remarkable when one considers how many bereaved and unhappy people visit graveyards with their thoughts focused on their deceased loved ones. However, wherever such a vacuum of sightings exists, it seems the legend-making capacity of human beings may operate, creating stories. Given the prominence of St Nicholas's church on the hillside going down to Brighton the growth of popular ghost tales was perhaps inevitable.

The story of the ghost ship visible out at sea every 17 May is linked with the foundation of the church. The legend – which has the hallmarks of a glorious fiction – maintains that on this date in the fourteenth century Sussex Earl de Warrenne was saved from death in a duel by a prayer uttered by his wife to St Nicholas. The intercession by the saint deflected what would otherwise have been a death blow from a sword wielded by Lord Pevensey, with whom de Warrenne was fighting. In gratitude for the saint's mercy the Earl Warrenne and his wife pledged to send their first born son on a pilgrimage to Byzantium when he was of age, in order to lay a relic, the Belt of St Nicholas, upon the tomb of the Blessed Virgin. It was a further condition that their son should not be married until the pilgrimage had been successfully performed. Regrettably as the years wore on the oath was forgotten and the eldest son Lord Manfred grew up and wed a Lady Edona on 17 May, the anniversary of the duel. Half-way through the wedding banquet an icy wind blew through the hall extinguishing the fire and candles. The whole party were stunned by a spectral vision revealing the history of the family and its broken promise. Appalled by the vision, Lord Manfred immediately postponed further nuptial celebrations, called for a ship and immediately set off to Byzantium to fulfil the pledge.

Exactly one year afterwards, a vessel flying Lord Manfred's flag was sighted off Worthing Point and the Warrennes set off to welcome his return. However, before it landed the ship struck a rock and capsized and all on board were drowned. Lady Edona collapsed and died on the spot and Earl Warrenne was so overcome with grief that he never smiled again. In remorse and piety he set about building St Nicholas's church, which also served as the resting spot for Lady Edona. At midnight on each 17 May, the ghostly form of Lord Manfred's vessel is said to appear out to sea and be visible from the churchyard.

Another story holds that a knight and his horse were buried in the churchyard. Local tradition credits the ghostly horse with emerging from a tomb in the churchyard every full moon for a canter. This story may be a garbled account of a genuine psychic manifestation since there are persistent stories of a phantom horseman in the churchyard. Such stories have been in circulation for well over thirty years, although first-hand witnesses have been hard to discover. In 1977, the then vicar the Revd Eackersley played down the stories, perhaps in the hope of discouraging curiosity seekers.

Over the years enthusiastic ghost hunters have claimed experiences in the churchyard. Some of the most extraordinary were those of a local man, Mr Dave Stringer of the Southern Area Paranormal Research Group, who gave an interview to the Brighton *Evening Argus* in February 1979. Mr Stringer described being with a group of friends in the churchyard, '...when a dreadful smell of sulphur overcame one of the group.' It would be tempting to dismiss this as auto-suggestion (or a broken drain) but the group also heard the sound of footsteps they were unable to explain. Even more peculiar was hearing conversations in which they had engaged in some forty-five minutes earlier being replayed to them. However, despite being equipped with an infrared camera and other gadgets the group were unable to penetrate the mysteries any further.

A correspondent to the *Evening Argus* in May 1999 reported that the horseman had been seen by a member of the Home Guard whilst on sentry duty during the Second World War. Guard duty was performed in twos after one man swore he had seen a white horse and rider 'glide over the gravestones'. Various proposals have been put forward as to the identity of the mysterious horseman, including a Saxon warrior. Other accounts have spoken of the appearance of a figure in Regency-era costume. These contradictions are hard to reconcile unless it is considered that the haunting is the 'idea pattern' of a rider on a horse that shapes and clothes itself in the subconscious mind of the witness, much like an external stimulus can trigger imagery in dreams.

One suggestion is that the apparition is linked with the brutal suppression of a military protest in 1795. The soldiers concerned were part of the Oxford Regiment which had established a camp to the west of St Nicholas's church. At the time Brighton held a garrison with troops stationed at a number of barracks around the town, including one in nearby Church Road. Soldiers from the Oxford Regiment complained about the quality of the bread and flour supplied to them. In protest they broke into a mill near their camp and also emptied a container of flour into a river, presumably to show their displeasure.

The military authorities reacted with severity, the offences being treated as cases of military mutiny. A court martial was duly held at the Castle Tavern in Brighton with the prisoners

St Nicholas' church.

paraded under guard through the town each day. The ringleaders, two soldiers named Cooke and Parish, were sentenced to death and four other men to 300 lashes each. These harsh sentences doubtless reflected the fear of sedition which was very much alive at the time, with the example of the French Revolution just across the Channel. Nonetheless, the harsh and disproportionate punishments led to an outpouring of sympathy from the townspeople of Brighton for the condemned men, who were marched over to Hove for execution by firing squad on 13 June 1795.

Most affected of all was the curate, the Revd Dring, who had to minister to the men before they died. He begged that the execution should not be carried out until he was safely out of earshot and promptly fled the scene. For their part, the two mutineers 'behaved with uncommon firmness and resignation' at the end, despite having two crude coffins displayed in front of them. However, despite the promise having been given to the Revd Dring to allow him time to leave, it seems the command to fire was either given prematurely, or the hapless curate failed to make good his escape with sufficient haste, for he was still within hearing range when the musket volley ended the lives of Cooke and Parish. The curate collapsed to the ground in horror and 'never after recovered the shock upon his nerves.' Meanwhile the still-bleeding bodies of the two executed men were hastily carried by fellow soldiers to Hove churchyard. So flimsy were the coffins provided that blood seeped through the wood, staining the tunics of the burial party. The bodies were interred close to the wall of Hove churchyard where they remained until restoration of the church in 1834. Could the rider on the horse be a messenger riding to inform the barracks or even the clergyman attempting to hasten from the scene of the execution?

The Clayton Railway Tunnel ghosts

The early days of railways in the Victorian era were blighted by many fatal train crashes. Many accidents were caused by corner-cutting and negligence by profiteers caught up in the railway mania which erupted across the country when the possibility of long-distance travel opened up to the population. One of the worst accidents of the period was the collision which occurred at the Clayton Tunnel, five miles outside of Brighton in 1861. The disaster occurred in spite of the tunnel having been fitted with a special telegraph and signalling system designed to prevent tunnel collisions. Victims of the crash have been said to haunt the tunnel ever since.

On the morning of 25 August 1861 three heavy passenger trains left Brighton after eight in the morning bound for Victoria in London, with an interval of five minutes between them. These were the Portsmouth Express, the *Brighton Excursion* and the *Brighton Ordinary* train. As the trains laboured over the chalk downs, the gap between all three narrowed. After the Portsmouth train, known as 'Pompey', passed through the tunnel a combination of signal failure and mistakes by the signalmen – one of whom had been on duty for twenty-four hours – led the engine driver of the following *Brighton Excursion* to stop and reverse his train back down the lengthy tunnel. The *Brighton Excursion* was about 250 yards from the mouth of the tunnel when it was struck at speed from behind by last of the three, the on-coming *Brighton Ordinary* train which was travelling at speed. A terrific detonation ran down the length of the tunnel and the guard in the rear of the *Brighton Excursion* leapt for his life as the *Ordinary* engine smashed through his van and collided with the rear coach.

The huge force of the impact arched the engine of the *Brighton Ordinary* up into the air until its chimney struck the tunnel roof. At the same time, the still-spinning wheels of the doomed engine mangled the roof of the crushed *Excursion* coach beneath it like scythe blades. To complete

Signalling equipment failed to avert the fatal Clayton tunnel crash of 1861.

the carnage, the furnace and pipes of the *Brighton Ordinary* then ruptured, sending down showers of hot coals and scalding steam upon the wrecked passenger coach beneath it. Twenty-three people died most horribly and 176 were injured in the wreck. The bodies of the victims were taken and laid out in the garden of the Gothic-style turreted house above the tunnel, which provided a temporary mortuary for the dead and a first aid station for the injured.

A subsequent enquiry by the Board of Trade brought much criticism upon the London, Brighton and South Coast Railway Company who owned the line. The incident also led to some improvements being brought to signalling at the Clayton and other tunnels – though unbelievably the owners were reluctant to improve the situation. Certainly, the tragedy led to no short-term improvements in safety on British railways, for over the next five years a further 209 people died in railway accidents across the UK and, in 1870, accidents on the Brighton line alone claimed a further twelve lives and nearly 200 injured. Although juries would often award large sums in compensation to victims and bereaved relatives, it was often said that the only winners from the slaughter were the lawyers.

The disaster was said to have 'cast a pall over the tunnel forever' and there have been rumours of haunting presences for many years. Further tragedies have boosted its grim reputation. In 1973 three Territorial Army soldiers on a map-reading exercise were killed in the tunnel and, in 2002, a man jumped from a train as it approached the entrance with fatal results.

What have been described as 'agonised groans' and cries and sounds of a crash have been heard issuing from the depths of the tunnel during the night, suggesting the re-enactment of the Clayton disaster. The cottage above the tunnel also has a reputation for being haunted, the phantom being known as the White Lady who is considered to be either a victim of the wreck or a woman searching for a missing relative. The cottage also had a reputation for being haunted by an invisible male presence, an entity dubbed 'Charlie', whose footsteps were heard in the building by a former tenant.

Sounds of a phantom train wreck are still reputedly heard today.

The Clayton disaster also provided an inspiration for one of Charles Dickens' most famous ghost stories, *The Signalman*. (Dickens himself was also to later witness a train wreck at first-hand.) Frequently anthologised and made into a powerful television play with the late Denholm Elliot in 1974, his story centres upon a haunted signalman at an isolated tunnel who maintains warning bells and wires designed to prevent collisions.

The stories of a haunting at Clayton Tunnel received national prominence in May 1996 when the cottage was put up for sale by Railtrack. Amid much joking that the cottage was 'a perfect home for train spotters and anoraks', the agent struck a more sombre note telling the *Daily Express*: 'I would advertise it for trainspotters. But most spotters would not be into all the ghost stuff. It would have to go to somebody who is a bit weird and wacky.'

Phantoms of the A23

Stories of road ghosts are found throughout Great Britain and many other countries, both in folklore and fact. Although it is rare indeed for the A23 leaving Brighton to be free of vehicles for any length of time, this stretch of road has nonetheless so many reports of what have been termed 'spectral pedestrians' since the end of the 1960s that it has become notorious as one of the most haunted roads in the country. Sightings have continued into the twenty-first century.

At Christmas 1976 Mr Dave Wright and his wife Joan were driving back from a seasonal visit to relatives in Birmingham when their headlights picked out a man in shirt sleeves staggering across the road. They thought he looked dazed and feared he may have been in an accident. He came so close that the Wrights feared that their vehicle might have hit him, so they immediately turned the car around and travelled back down the road. There was no trace of anyone to be seen. Mrs Wright recalled that she had found the whole incident eerie and that she had locked the car door before they had returned to the spot, '…something I never normally do'. She said: 'I felt a bit scared.' Subsequently, Mrs Wright learned that other people had seen strange figures 'drifting across the road'.

Their sighting came less than a month after Mr Patrick Geary and his wife had seen a woman in a white mackintosh step along the same stretch of road on a rainy night in early December 1976. They had seen the figure step into the road and straight into the path of their car. The couple felt they must have collided with the figure but there was no-one to be found. The local *Evening Argus* reported that sightings went back at least eight years and also included another figure in a red coat. Other stories spoke of a limping blonde woman near Pyecombe, said to be that of a young woman killed in a motorcycle accident. Yet other stories told of 'a young man in cricketing clothes' and 'a tall thin woman in a cape and hood', accompanied by 'the figure of a child similarly dressed' or 'a small child in a small duffel coat' – unusual because few road ghosts seem to be of children, despite the numbers who die on roads. By the end of 1977 the ghosts on the A23 had become so well known that they merited a mention in Jack Hallam's *The Ghosts Who's Who*.

Another sighting along the same road occurred in 1992 when three men travelling by road to Brighton decided to pull into the former Queen's Head pub which stood at Bolney. As their car crossed into the car park a woman in a grey dress suddenly appeared in front of the car. The driver braked sharply but it was too late to avert a collision, and the driver felt a sickening thud as the car skidded across the road. The shocked men got out the car to find no-one. The woman had completely vanished and, in spite of a search by both the men and the police, the mystery remained unsolved.

A special category to describe such phantoms has even been established, that of 'Spectral Pedestrian'. Realistic human apparitions are seen crossing or standing in a road in the path of on-coming motorists using the highway. Sometimes the figure is immediately recognisable as an apparition by its movement or appearance, whilst in other cases it is taken to be a living human person until disappearing. As with the story of the incident at Bolney there are many cases of motorists reporting apparent collisions with such figures only to discover no physical traces of any person.

Another Christmas-time ghost sighting on the A23 – this time of a dog – came in December 1996. Local taxi driver Leonard Bish reported seeing a ghostly golden Labrador. 'I was just driving along when suddenly I saw this dog just walk slowly out in front of me. I had to swerve hard to avoid it'. Mr Bish also knew of at least one other person who had seen the dog and had driven straight through it. Further sightings came in February 1997, prompting suggestions that the dog was that of a pet golden Labrador which had belonged to a local farmer and had been killed on the road ten years before.

Ghost sightings along the road have continued into the twenty-first century according to details now posted on the internet, on websites devoted to ghosts and hauntings. Among recent witnesses have been a nurse travelling home to Brighton late one night who encountered a figure in the road which – like all the others – inexplicably vanished.

The haunted barn

One of the most fascinating stories of a haunting near Brighton appeared in the *Hove and Brighton Gazette* in April 1934. The paper recorded the experience of a local shepherd at a barn used for lambing at West Blatchington Farm, close to the old windmill and the church of St Peter. The shepherd had seen the ghost of a woman on three different nights at Easter time the previous year (1933) when he had been up after midnight tending to ewes and lambs in a 400-year-old barn. The shepherd entered the barn with his collie dog waiting outside, using a storm lantern for illumination. Soon afterwards his lamp was mysteriously extinguished, followed by a rattling of the doors and shutters, and from the large window at the end of the barn came a bright light and the white-clothed form of a woman appeared. The shepherd saw the figure float along the side of one wall inside the barn and vanish through a door at the opposite end, into a dark room. During the appearance the collie outside the barn barked furiously and the sheep inside huddled together in fear as the glowing form glided by. The shepherd struggled to re-light his lamp but was unable to do so until he left the barn.

On the following night the same manifestation was repeated, the light again being mysteriously extinguished. On the third and fourth nights nothing occurred, but on the fifth night the apparition of the woman appeared and the lamp was again quenched. This proved too much for the shepherd who thereafter refused to work in the barn. As a result a new shed was constructed to accommodate the sheep and lambs.

The newspaper gave the apparition the title of the 'White Lady of West Blatchington' and enthusiastically pursued the story in the following weeks. Their zeal was not appreciated by the shepherd who fiercely refused requests for an interview, having been pestered by curiosity seekers following all the publicity. 'If you want to see the ghost, go to the barn and see her for yourself', he angrily told a reporter before slamming his door.

Nonetheless, the journalists remained impressed by his story and obtained permission to hold a ghost hunt themselves at the barn. This occurred overnight during the week beginning 21

Above: *A barn close to West Blatchington Mill was the scene of the strange apparition of the White Lady in 1933.*

Left: *The shepherd's experience was sensationalised as 'the White Lady of West Blatchington' in the press and prompted a ghost hunt by journalists.*

Mr Henty (right) and his ghost-hunting team in 1951.

April 1934 and the story appeared the following Saturday. Unfortunately, their efforts were in vain. Their cameras resulted in blank photographs, although they did obtain some wonderfully atmospheric pictures by time exposure at midnight.

No further reports of the White Lady were received but the paper nonetheless considered 'This district seems well stocked with ghosts' and recorded the story of another haunted building called Gibbet Barn, not far away. The barn stood on the site of a gibbet from which the body of a local young man was hung, following his execution for robbing a mail coach. His bones were later collected by his grieving mother and his ghost was said to haunt the spot.

Mr Henty, the 1950s ghost buster

One reason why progress in our understanding of ghosts is so limited is that scientific ghost hunting is just over a century old. Prior to the 1880s the ghost hunter was often indistinguishable from the spirit raiser or necromancer and until the 1930s most efforts at ghost investigation took place in the séance room, rather than in haunted premises. However, from the 1920s onwards efforts to investigate ghosts with scientific equipment became more common. The leading champion of this approach was the controversial and publicity-conscious Harry Price (1881–1948) who lived at Pulborough in Sussex. Price brought psychical research to the wider public and encouraged the use of instruments and cameras at haunted locations, in the hope of capturing evidence of phantoms.

After Price's death the technical approach to ghost hunting languished but in 1950 national news was made on account of the efforts of a Mr Ted Henty to revive the scientific approach. A former police officer, Mr Henty established a group called the Sussex Ghost Hunters who

THEY FIGHT BOGIES WITH SCIENCE

Ghost Busters

By JOHN ENNIS

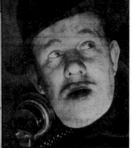

Ted Henty spots a ghost — and broadcasts his feelings!

THE guests were leaving. As they prepared to step out into the storm, a weird sound of clanking chains echoed through the house.

They held their breath, then: "It's our ghost again," the hosts explained with a worried smile.

That was too simple an explanation for the guests Ted and Elphine Henty, of Reigate Road, Brighton. They took off their coats, and began a ghost hunt on the spot.

They stayed until 5 a.m. on that stormy January morning three years ago. They found nothing to explain the mysterious clanking. But they didn't give up.

"We went back four times," Ted Henty, 47, told me last week. "We searched every inch of that house — and we found the 'ghost.'"

'Magic eye' camera

A BRANCH on a tree at the side of the house, blown by the wind when it was in a certain direction, caught in a piece of corrugated iron. Jerkily it sprang back, one corrugation at a time, sending an amplified "clank" echoing through the house.

And that is how the Sussex Ghost Hunters began.

"If one ghost has a material explanation," thought Ted, "then others will, too. And that explanation can be found—providing there is somebody keen enough to look for it long enough and hard enough."

He found there were a dozen people in Brighton keen to become ghost-hunters. They got together and worked out an elaborate set of ghost-finding equipment.

It includes—

Walkie-talkie sets, so that the ghost hunters can speak to a central control room while they are

dispersed around the house they are investigating;

Recording apparatus, to record all unusual sounds; yards of wire to wire up for sound a whole house if necessary; adhesive tape to stick over "pictures that move";

A "Magic Eye" infra-red camera, to take photographs in the dark; torches, felt overshoes, flasks of coffee—and a truncheon to deal with practical jokers (Ted Henty is an ex-policeman).

All the equipment is carried to the job in a 14 hp Fordson truck. And the Sussex Ghost Hunters never refuse a call for help. Even if it comes in the middle of the night—hail, rain or snow. No charge is made, but if the client likes to cover expenses it means the team is not always out of pocket.

Ghost banging on door

ALL they insist on is that the house-holders give them written permission to investigate, and that the local police are told of their activities. An understandable precaution when some of the team might spend half the

night prowling among the chimney-pots.

Their only reward is the satisfaction of clearing up one mystery after another.

"And do you know," exclaimed Ted, "we find most people are disappointed when we tell them they have no ghost after all."

One client who was relieved rather than disappointed was an old woman who lived in the ground floor flat of a converted Regency house in Brighton.

In terror she called Henty at eleven o'clock one night. "It's here again, it's here again," she moaned into the telephone.

"What is?" he asked.

"The ghost," gasped the old lady.

The team snapped into action. Henty arrived first and heard the noise that worried the woman.

It was as if somebody in armour was walking along the corridor and banging on her door.

"It happens at the same time every night," she told him.

She was right. It happened every night at the time that the porter, who had his room in the basement, was ready to go home. Before leaving it was his habit to wash under a running tap. The tap had a loose washer. A plunger that thus banged up and down was frightening the old woman on the floor above out of her wits.

That case was fairly easy to close. For the "ghosts" that are harder to trace, the hunters have worked out an intricate routine of investigation.

First, a check is made on the client if there is time. They have to beware of cranks.

Four women in team

THEN the whole house is wired for sound after one room has been ear-marked as a control centre. All doors and windows are sealed. Members of the team —four are women—are stationed at key points inside, outside, on top of and underneath the house.

But first the pulse rate and temperature of each is taken to ensure he or she is fit to face any shocks that are coming.

All these precautions were taken in the case of the moving pictures.

Every member of a household was scared to sleep in a certain room. Reason? There were faint tapping sounds during the night and every morning the pictures on the wall were awry. The family were sure they had a poltergeist.

The ghost-busters taped the pictures to the wall. They trained a "magic eye" camera on one of the pictures and waited.

Next morning they had a picture of—birds. Through the open window they had been flying into the "haunted" room, standing on the top edge of the picture and pecking at the wall paper to get at some bird delicacy in the paste behind. So much for the poltergeist.

Two nights a week for three weeks it took the hunters to find the cause of a sound as if a tunnel was being dug under one house. The answer—rats behind the skirting board.

A retired bank manager was on the point of selling his bungalow because he and his wife were terrified by the sound of machinery running under the floor. Three nights' work told the Ghost Hunters that the sound was the humming of telephone wires, queerly amplified by the structure of the bungalow.

A farm worker and his wife believed they could hear water being drawn from their well

every night. Henty's boys and girls said there was nothing to worry about—it was pigeons billing and cooing under the eaves.

Leaking pipe was clue

FOUR people reported separately the ghostly knockings heard regularly in one old house. The knockings were traced to a leaking pipe, dripping in the rafters. A piece of insulation tape round the pipe laid that "ghost."

Forty-five cases the Ghost Hunters have tackled. They have solved 43 of them and found a material reason for the "hauntings."

Two remain unsolved. One is the apparition of a woman in medieval costume; the other of a man in Stuart dress.

Ted Henty has seen the male ghost himself, and has made a recording of what he saw while he was seeing it.

They are hoping that new apparatus designed by Dudley Gamble-Jones, 48-year-old inventor member of the team, will help them to find a scientific reason for these visions.

There is one question everybody wants to ask the Ghost Hunters. After all this, do they believe in ghosts?

"We don't know," they answer. "We go into each new case with an open mind."

Fitting the cellar of a haunted house with a walkie-talkie set

An extract from Reynolds News.

formed a team of investigators to look into a number of haunted properties in the Brighton area, in the late 1940s and early 1950s. Mr Henty was an impressive character. One journalist stated, 'Mr Henty, although a gentleman, is a fearsome enough challenger to any ghost. He has an old-fashioned film villain moustache and piercing blue eyes that thrust at you from under aggressive brows. He meticulously placed his hands together and talked about ghosts in a well-modulated voice.'

Like Price twenty years before, Mr Henty courted publicity in the local and national press. 'They fight bogies with science', was a headline in an article in *Reynolds News* in June 1950, referring to them as 'Ghost Busters', perhaps one of the earliest uses of the term. The group was equipped with, 'walkie talkie sets so that the ghost hunters can speak to a central control room while they are dispersed around the house they are investigating… Recording apparatus to record all unusual sounds; yards of wire to wire up for sound a whole house if necessary, adhesive tape to stick over pictures that move… a "Magic Eye" infrared camera to take photographs in the dark; torches, felt overshoes.' Perhaps humorously the group also had a truncheon 'to deal with practical jokers' (this was before offensive weapon legislation was passed).

Unfortunately, precise locations are hard to identify from the reports but it is clear they were very active in Brighton and the surrounding area. The group maintained that it had solved forty-three out of forty-five cases which it had looked into; natural causes such as bad plumbing explained an alleged ghost in a converted Regency house in Brighton. Birds, rats and the amplified humming of telephone wires had been found in other alleged hauntings. A farm worker and his wife believed they could hear water being drawn from a well every night; the explanation was found to be 'pigeons billing and cooing under the eves'.

The two unexplained cases were a woman in medieval costume and a man in Stuart dress. Ted Henty had seen the male ghost for himself and made a recording of what he saw. In September 1951 the Sussex Ghost Hunters held a twelve hour vigil at an old farmhouse near Shoreham, accompanied by journalists from the national and local press. As well as using electrical equipment they also attempted dowsing by means of a pendulum. Nothing was conclusively recorded but they were convinced that there were genuine manifestations in the property.

In October 1953, the Sussex Ghost Hunters investigated a 200 year old house near an old manor house on the Wick Estate, near Hove. The ghosts of the house – which had stood empty for most of the previous twenty years – had reputedly scared three caretakers and some soldiers who had been inside. Paint bottles inside had been moved out of locked rooms, heavy corks were taken out of acid containers and locked doors found open. An apparition of a man and a woman had been seen. Mr Henty and his team were filmed by *Pathe News* dealing with the poltergeist. It seems on this occasion they suffered problems with equipment failure of the sort which have been encountered in ghost hunting by technical means in more recent years.

Did Mr Henty's team ever successfully record a ghost? Regrettably, no more accounts have been found concerning their persistent efforts in the cause of psychic research. But clearly the Sussex Ghost Hunters were convinced that genuine ghosts were waiting to be discovered in the Brighton area – a position which remains just as true today.

Other local titles published by Tempus

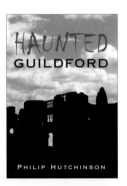

Haunted Guildford

PHILIP HUTCHINSON

Haunted Guildford contains a chilling range of ghostly accounts: from tales of a piano-playing spirit at Guildford museum and a spectral monk-like figure who wanders up Friary street, to stories of a poltergeist at The Three Pigeons public house and sightings of a ghostly woman on Whitmoor common, this selection is sure to appeal to anyone interested in the supernatural history of the area

0 7524 3826 3

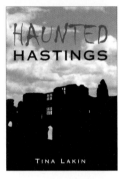

Haunted Hastings

TINA LAKIN

From the haunted staircase at Hastings library in Claremont and the singing spectre of Hastings College to the mysterious witches' footsteps in the Stag Inn and the phantom coach and horses that gallop up the High Street on a dark winter's night, this phenomenal gathering of ghostly goings-on is bound to captivate those interested in haunted Hastings.

0 7524 3827 1

Haunted Kent

JANET CAMERON

Haunted Kent contains spooky stories from around the county, including the hunchbacked monk at Boughton Malherbe, the black dog of Leeds and the well-known tale of Lady Blanche of Rochester Castle. This fascinating collection of strange sightings and happenings in the county's streets, churches, public houses and country lanes will interest anyone wanting to know why Kent is known as the most haunted county in England.

0 7524 3605 8

Haunted Winchester

MATTHEW FELDWICK

This chilling selection includes tales of spectral monks at Winchester Cathedral and phantom horses in the Cathedral Close, as well as stories of the Eclipse Inn where Dame Alice Lisle, condemned by Judge Jefferies, still walks. This collection of spooky stories and frightening phenomena will fascinate anyone interested in the supernatural sightings of the streets of Winchester.

0 7524 3846 8

If you are interested in purchasing other books published by Tempus, or in case you have difficulty finding any Tempus books in your local bookshop, you can also place orders directly through our website

www.tempus-publishing.com